Journey in a Journal:
A Personalized Cookbook for Your Cooking Journey

Chef Lissa Turner

Copyright © 2020 Lissa Turner

All rights reserved. No part of this book may be reproduced or transmitted in any form or by any means, electronic or mechanical, including photocopying, recording or by any information storage and retrieval system without permission in writing from the publisher.

Elle Cee Tee—Madison, WI
ISBN: 978-0-578-80523-8
Title: *Journey in a Journal*
Author: Lissa Turner
Digital distribution | 2020
Paperback | 2020

This is a work of fiction. The characters, names, incidents, places, and dialogue are products of the author's imagination, and are not to be construed as real.

Dedication

I'd like to dedicate this to every person along my Journey, however, space is limited and it would be quite a long list to include everyone that has been along with me on my food path and Journey.

Mostly, though, I do have to specifically mention my Husband, Josh and my kiddo's, Rebecca "Reba" and Jacob "JD", who have been begging me to write a book for years. Without their support and extra set of eyes, this would not be possible.

Introduction

Ingredients:
Pen, Pencil, Markers, or Highlighter
Bookmark
Basic Knowledge
Imagination
Willingness to Experiment and try New Things

Directions:

This is a notebook or journal for the inspiring chef or ambitious home cook. I really want you to experiment with the ingredients and quantities you have on hand. I'd love it for you to keep notes and ideas right on the pages of this book. There are not many specific amounts or quantities. This is for you to decide. Please take my knowledge and ideas and transform them into your own! If you hate mushrooms- leave them out. If you love garlic- try shallots or add more garlic. If you've never used sesame oil or seeds- try them now. Make this cookbook your cookbook!
   Thank You
   Chef Lissa Turner

Table of Contents- Chapter 1

Beef Chili 1
Mexican Meatloaf 2
Beef Stroganoff 3

Parmesan Chicken Meatballs 4
Waldorf Chicken Salad 5
Turkey Meatloaf 6

Dill Salmon with Capers 7
Shrimp Scampi over Pasta 8
Citrus glazed Salmon 9

Cajun Red Beans and Rice 10
Pork Tenderloin with Apples 11
Baked Ziti with Italian Sausage 12

Quiche Lorraine 13
Potato, Broccoli, and Pepper Jack Egg Casserole 14
Basil and Cherry Tomato Quiche 15

Black Bean and Vegetable Enchilada Casserole 16
Vegetable Frittata 17
Tri-Color Bell Pepper Baked Ziti 18

Leek and Potato Soup 19
Chicken Wild Rice Soup 20
Shrimp Pasta Salad 21

Auntie Lissa's Quick Menu Facts- Chapter 1

Is Ground Chicken Nutritious?
Calories Per Serving: 140
Cholesterol: 95 mg
Fat: 1 g
Sodium: 100 mg
Protein: 23 g

What is a Caper?
Simple Definition:
Pickled Flower Buds

Cajun Seasoning-
3 T Paprika, 2 T Kosher Salt,
2 T Garlic Powder, 1 T Ground
Black Pepper, 1 T Ground White
Pepper, 1 T Onion Powder,
1 T Oregano, 1 T Cayenne,
and ½ T Thyme.

Shrimp Sizing Chart-
Jumbo: 21-25 per pound
Extra Large: 26-30
Large: 31-35
Medium Large: 36-40
Tiny: 71 + per pound

What's the difference- Heavy Cream and Heavy Whipping Cream?
NONE!!

Quick Homemade BBQ-
1 ½ c Brown Sugar, 1 ½ c Ketchup,
½ c Red Wine Vinegar, ½ c Water
1 T Worcestershire, 2 ½ T Dry
Mustard, 2 t Paprika, Salt & Pepper,
and a Dash of Tabasco.

Green v. Red v. Yellow Bell Peppers-
Maturity.
Green to Yellow to Red = Bitter to Sweet.

Cooking Wine v. Drinking Wine-
Cooking Wine is a salty flavor enhancer and Drinking Wine is a finer and stronger in flavor. I prefer to cook with cheaper Drinking Wine.

The Lorraine in Quiche Lorraine-
Named after the Lorraine region in France. Made with Cheese, Bacon, and Onion.

Popular Pasta-
Fusilli, Spaghetti, Fettuccine, Linguine, Penne, Cannelloni, Tagliatelle, Farfalle, Tortellini, Rigatoni…...

Russet v. Idaho Potatoes-
Russets are grown in many states. Idaho are only grown in Idaho. Russet is the most well-known potato grown in ID.

Coarse v. Table Salt-
Coarse Salt is large crystals or granules. Table Salt is uniform crystals and mainly used for baking and light seasoning.

Beef Chili

Olive Oil
Onion, diced
Green Bell Pepper, diced
Garlic, minced
Ground Beef
Diced Tomatoes
Dark Red Kidney Beans, rinsed & drained

Beef Stock
Tomato Paste
Chili Powder
Cumin
Oregano
Salt & Pepper

Heat Olive Oil in a stock pot. Sauté Onion and Green Pepper. Add Garlic and brown Ground Beef. When Beef is browned, add Tomatoes, Paste, Beans, Herbs, and Spices.
Thin Chili to desired consistency with Beef Stock. Reduce again, if needed.

Notes/Journal:

Optional Ingredients:
Red Pepper Flakes
Top with diced Onion before serving
Black Beans
Corn

Sour Cream
Top with shredded Cheddar Cheese before serving
Light Red Kidney Beans

Optional Method:
Place ingredients in a crockpot for 4-6 hours.

Sides:
Corn Bread
Tortilla Chips

Homemade Bread Loaf
Corn Chips

_____

_____

_____

_____

_____

Mexican Meatloaf

Egg
Breadcrumbs
Onion, diced
Chili Powder
Cumin

Salt & Pepper
Ground Beef
Ground Pork
Sharp Cheddar, shredded
Taco Sauce

Preheat the oven to 350 degrees F.
Combine all the ingredients except Cheddar and Taco Sauce. Form into a loaf and place in a lightly oiled loaf pan. Top loaf with Taco Sauce.
Bake for 30 minutes. Top the Meatloaf with Cheddar Cheese and bake for an additional 10 minutes.

Notes/Journal:

Optional Ingredients:
Taco Seasoning
Picante Sauce
Salsa
Tabasco

_____
_____
_____
_____
_____
_____
_____
_____
_____

Beef Stroganoff

Beef Tenderloin, thinly sliced
Mushrooms, sliced
Onions, sliced
Garlic, minced
Butter
Beef Stock

Salt & Pepper
Flour
Worcestershire Sauce
Sour Cream
Egg Noodles, prepared

Cook Mushrooms, Onions, and Garlic in Butter in a sauté pan. Remove from the pan.
Cook Beef in the sauté pan. Stir in Stock, Salt & Pepper, and Worcestershire Sauce.
Heat to boiling, reduce heat, cover, and simmer.
Stir ½ c of Stock with ¼ c Flour. Stir mixture into Beef mixture. Add Onions and Mushrooms.
Heat to boiling, stirring.
Remove pan from heat. Add Sour Cream. Stir. Serve over Noodles.

Notes/Journal:

Optional Ingredients:
Portabella Mushrooms, sliced

Substitutions: Substitute Coconut Milk to make lactose free and olive oil for butter. Some Worcestershire Sauces are not gluten free.

_____

_____

Parmesan Chicken Meatballs

Ground Chicken	Frozen Spinach, thawed and dried
Egg	Garlic, minced
Breadcrumbs	Can San Marzano Tomatoes
Italian Seasoning	Mozzarella, shredded
Parsley	Salt & Pepper
Parmesan Cheese, grated	Olive Oil

Preheat the oven to 350 degrees F.
Combine all the ingredients except for ½ Parmesan, Mozzarella, and San Marzano Tomatoes. Form Meatballs with Meat mixture. Place in a heated, lightly Oiled sauté pan. Cover Meatballs with Tomatoes. Sprinkle with Mozzarella and remaining Parmesan.
Bake in the preheated oven until the Meatballs are cooked through and the Cheese is melted.

Notes/Journal:
A heavy cast iron skillet is an ideal pan for this dish. Both for cooking and serving.

_____

_____

_____

Waldorf Chicken Salad

Walnuts, chopped
Chicken Breast, cooked and diced
Grapes, halved
Apples, diced
Celery, diced
Mayonnaise
Salt & Pepper

Mix all ingredients and chill until serving.

Notes/Journal:

_____
_____
_____
_____
_____
_____
_____
_____
_____
_____
_____
_____

Turkey Meatloaf

Onion, finely chopped
Ground Turkey
Red Bell Pepper, finely chopped
Breadcrumbs
Salt & Pepper
Egg
Thyme
Ketchup

Preheat the oven to 350 degrees F.
Combine all ingredients. Shape into loaf and place in a lightly greased loaf pan.
Top Meatloaf with Ketchup and bake for 30-40 minutes.
Bake until cooked through.

Notes/Journal:

_____
_____
_____
_____
_____
_____
_____
_____
_____

Dill Salmon with Capers

Salmon Portions
Salt & Pepper
Dill, stemmed and chopped or dried

Capers, drained
Olive Oil
Stock

Season Salmon Portions generously with Dill, Salt & Pepper. Heat sauté pan with Olive Oil until hot. Sear top of Salmon in Oil. Flip Portion over. Add a small amount of Stock and Capers to the pan and finish Fish in the oven. Serve hot.

Notes/Journal:

_____
_____
_____
_____
_____
_____
_____
_____
_____
_____
_____

Shrimp Scampi with Pasta

Linguine, cooked and drained
Butter
Shallots, sliced
Garlic, minced
Shrimp, raw, peeled, and deveined

Salt & Pepper
Stock
White Wine
Lemons, quartered in wedges

Heat Butter in a sauté pan. Add half the Lemon wedges and sauté the Shallots and Garlic. Add the Wine and reduce.
Add Stock and reduce further. Season the Shrimp and cook in the liquid until just pink. Discard sautéed Lemon Wedges.
Add cooked Linguine and heat through.
Serve with remaining Lemon wedges as garnish

Notes/Journal:

Watch the Salt. Depending on the stock or wine you choose, the liquid will become very salty fast.

_____
_____
_____
_____
_____

Citrus glazed Salmon

Salmon Portions
Orange, slice half and wedge remaining
Lemon, wedged
Soy Sauce

Olive Oil
Brown Sugar
Salt & Pepper

Preheat the oven to 350-degree F.
Season Portions with Salt & Pepper. Heat Olive Oil in a sauté pan add Orange and Lemon Wedges. When HOT, sear the Portion tops and flip. Sprinkle the top of Salmon with Brown Sugar. Place Orange slices on top of Brown Sugar and splash with Soy Sauce.
Bake until Salmon is cooked through.

Notes/Journal:

It does not take Salmon very long to cook through. If you use a loin section from the Salmon it will take a touch longer than the fillet or tail portion. It should take just under 10 minutes to just under 15 minutes.

_____
_____
_____
_____
_____

Cajun Red Beans and Rice

Olive Oil	Garlic, minced
Spicy Ground Italian Sausage OR	Can Red Beans, rinsed and drained
Sausage Links, sliced	Can Diced Tomatoes
Onion, diced	Stock
Bell Pepper, diced	Salt & Pepper
Celery, diced	Rice, cooked
Cajun Seasoning	

Heat Olive Oil in a sauté pan. Sauté Onions, Bell Pepper, and Celery until soft. Add and brown the Sausage. To the mixture add Garlic, Cajun Seasoning, Salt & Pepper. Mix well. Add Diced Tomatoes, Beans, and Stock. Increase heat. Once the Beans and Meat mixture boil, add Rice. Reduce heat and simmer until sauce reduces and thickens.
Remove from heat and serve.

Notes/Journal:

_____
_____
_____
_____
_____

Pork Tenderloin with Apples

Pork Tenderloin
Salt & Pepper
Olive Oil
Onion, sliced

Apple, sliced or diced
Sage Leaf
Dijon Mustard
Stock

Preheat the oven to 350 degrees F.
Rub Tenderloin with Dijon Mustard, Salt & Pepper, and Sage Leaf. Heat Olive Oil in a sauté pan. Sear Pork on all sides, in the meantime sauté Onions, Apples and additional Sage. After Pork is seared and Apple/Onion mixture is golden, add Stock to deglaze the pan. Place the pan in the oven and bring the Pork to temperature before resting and serving.

Notes/Journal:
Honeycrisp or Golden Delicious Apples pair very nicely with Pork.

_____
_____
_____
_____
_____

Baked Ziti

Olive Oil
Onion, diced
Green Bell Pepper, diced
Garlic, minced
Italian Sausage or Links
Can Diced Tomatoes
Tomato Sauce

Basil, stemmed and ribboned or dried
Salt & Pepper
Ziti Pasta, cooked and drained
Ricotta Cheese
Parmesan Cheese, shredded
Mozzarella Cheese, shredded

Preheat the oven to 350 degrees F.
Prepare Tomato Sauce with the Olive Oil, Onion, Green Pepper, Garlic, Italian Sausage, Diced Tomatoes, Tomato Sauce, Basil, Salt & Pepper.
Mix Ziti, Ricotta, Tomato Sauce, ½ Mozzarella, and ½ Parmesan. Pour mixture into baking dish. Top with remaining Cheeses.
Bake in the oven for 30 minutes or until bubbly.

Notes/Journal:

Ricotta Cheeses come in part-skim, whole milk, light, low fat, and fat free. This refers to the fat content. Part skim is very popular however, I prefer whole milk Ricotta
.

_____

_____

Quiche Lorraine

Pie Crust
Bacon, cooked and crumbled
Heavy Cream
Salt & Pepper

Chives, chopped finely or dried
Gruyere or Swiss Cheese, shredded
Eggs

Preheat the oven to 350 degrees F.
In a mixing bowl whisk Heavy Cream, Eggs, Salt & Pepper.
Place Bacon, Chives, and Cheese in Pie Crust. Pour Eggs into Pie Crust.
Bake in the oven for 30-40 minutes until the center is set and firm. Cool in the pan on a wire rack.

Notes/Journal:
Turkey Bacon may be substituted for the Bacon.

_____
_____
_____
_____
_____
_____
_____
_____
_____
_____
_____

Potato, Broccoli and Pepper Jack Cheese Egg Casserole

Hash Browns, thawed
Broccoli Florets
Ham, diced
Red Bell Pepper, diced
Onion, diced
Garlic, minced
Pepper Jack, shredded

Sharp Cheddar Cheese, shredded
Butter
Eggs
Milk
Sour Cream
Parsley
Salt & Pepper

Preheat the oven to 350 degrees F.
Sauté the Red Bell Pepper, Onion, and Garlic in Butter. Combine Potatoes, Ham, and ½ of each of the Cheeses. Spread ½ of the Potato mixture into a lightly greased baking dish. Top the mixture with the Broccoli. Add the Bell Pepper/Onions to the baking dish. Finish the pan with the remaining Potatoes.
Whisk together Eggs, Milk, Sour Cream, Salt & Pepper. Pour over the casserole. Sprinkle with Parsley and remaining Cheese.
Bake covered for 30 minutes. Uncover and bake for an additional 30-40 minutes. Cool 10 minutes before serving.

Notes/Journal:
This recipe can be made ahead and frozen. You can also split it between 2 or 3 baking dishes.

Basil and Cherry Tomato Quiche

Pie Crust
Fresh Basil, stems removed and roughly chopped
Cherry Tomatoes, halved
Heavy Cream
Eggs
Mozzarella, shredded
Salt & Pepper

Preheat the oven to 350 degrees F.
Whisk together the Eggs, Heavy Cream, Salt & Pepper. In Pie Crust, layer the Cheese, followed by the Basil. Top with the Cherry Tomatoes and the remaining Cheese.
Pour Egg over Quiche and bake for 30-40 minutes.

Notes/Journal:

For presentation consideration: Pour the Egg mixture before placing the Cherry Tomatoes on top. Place the Cherry Tomatoes on top in a pattern or design.

_____
_____
_____
_____
_____
_____
_____
_____
_____
_____

Black Bean and Vegetable Enchilada Casserole

Zucchini, peeled and small dice
Green Onions, sliced
Cilantro, stemmed and chopped
Garlic, minced
Cheddar Cheese, shredded
Corn

Tortillas
Enchilada Sauce
Black Beans, drained and rinsed
Green Chilis
Olive Oil
Salt & Pepper

Preheat the oven to 350 degrees F.
Heat Olive Oil in a sauté pan. Sauté Zucchini, Green Onions, and Garlic. Reduce heat, stir in Cilantro, Corn, Black Beans, Green Chilis, Salt & Pepper, and a few tablespoons of Enchilada Sauce.
Spoon a few tablespoons of Enchilada Sauce into a lightly greased baking dish. Place Tortillas in a single layer on the bottom of the pan followed by the Vegetables and Cheddar. Spoon Enchilada Sauce onto Cheese. Repeat layers until just shy of the top of the dish. Top the dish with remaining Enchilada Sauce and Cheddar Cheese.
Bake in the oven for 30 minutes or until bubbly and Cheese is melted. Cool slightly before serving

Notes/Journal:

Consider substituting Salsa Verde for the Enchilada Sauce. Also, consider adding a few tablespoons of Sour Cream to the Vegetable filling. You may freeze this dish however, it does taste the best fresh.

Vegetable Frittata

Butter
Red Potatoes, thinly sliced
Green Onions, thinly sliced
Roma Tomatoes, thinly sliced
Spinach, loosely chopped and stems removed

Fresh Basil, loosely chopped and stems removed
Garlic, minced
Eggs
Parmesan, shredded
Salt & Pepper

Heat oven to 350 degrees F.
Place 1 tablespoon of Butter in a baking dish in the heated oven. When melted, place sliced Potatoes in a single layer in the bottom of the pan. Season Potatoes with Salt & Pepper.
Bake until Potatoes are soft. Add another tablespoon of butter to the pan.
Add Green Onions to the baking dish. Bake until soft.
Pull the dish from the oven. Layer ½ the Cheese, Spinach, Basil, Garlic, Salt & Pepper.
Top with remaining Cheese and Tomatoes.
Whisk Eggs and pour over Vegetables.
Bake for 30-40 minutes or until Frittata is set and firm. Cool slightly before serving

Notes/Journal:

_____
_____
_____
_____
_____
_____
_____
_____
_____

Tri-Color Bell Pepper Baked Ziti

Olive Oil
Onion, diced
Green Bell Pepper, diced
Red Bell Pepper, diced
Yellow/Orange Bell Pepper, diced
Garlic, minced
Can Diced Tomatoes
Tomato Sauce- see below

Basil, stems removed and chopped or dried
Salt & Pepper
Ziti Pasta, cooked and drained
Ricotta Cheese
Parmesan Cheese, shredded
Mozzarella Cheese, shredded

Preheat the oven to 350 degrees F.
Prepare Tomato Sauce with the Olive Oil, Onion, Bell Peppers, Garlic, Diced Tomatoes, Tomato Sauce, Basil, and Salt & Pepper.
Mix Ziti, ½ each of the Cheeses, Tomato Sauce, and Ricotta. Pour into a lightly greased baking dish.
Top with the remaining Cheese.
Bake for 30 minutes or until bubbly and Cheese is melted.

Notes/Journal:

Adjust this recipe to **Stuffed Shells** or **Manicotti** quickly. Cook Pasta to the directions on the box. Stuff the Shells or Manicotti with a mixture of Ricotta, Parmesan, Mozzarella, and Basil. Place stuffed Pasta in a baking dish. Prepare a Tomato Sauce with the sautéed Vegetables, Garlic and Tomato Products. Pour Sauce over stuffed Pasta and top with ½ c of Mozzarella and ¼ c of Parmesan. Bake for 30 minutes or until bubbly and Cheese is melted.

_____
_____
_____
_____
_____
_____
_____
_____

Leek and Potato Soup

Leeks, cleaned and thinly sliced
Butter
Thyme
Salt & Pepper
Garlic, minced
Cornstarch Slurry
Stock
Half and Half
Celery, diced
Carrots, diced

Sauté Leeks in Butter, Thyme, Garlic, Salt & Pepper. Add Celery and Carrots. Sauté until soft. Add Potatoes and Stock. Bring to a boil and reduce the Soup to a brisk simmer until Potatoes are soft but firm. Bring back up to a boil and slowly whisk in the Cornstarch Slurry.

Reduce the heat and thin the soup back down with half and half until desired consistency

Notes/Journal:
Heavy Cream or Milk can be used instead of Half and Half.

_____
_____
_____
_____
_____
_____
_____
_____

Chicken and Wild Rice Soup

Chicken, roasted and diced OR
Ground Chicken, browned
Onion, diced
Carrots, diced
Celery, diced

Garlic, Minced
Wild Rice, prepared
Chicken Stock
Salt & Pepper
Thyme

Sauté Onions, Carrots, and Celery in hot Olive Oil until soft. Add Garlic and Chicken. Quickly stir. Add Stock, Wild Rice, and Seasoning. Bring to a boil. Reduce to a simmer.
Simmer until flavors meld. Serve.

Notes/Journal:

_____
_____
_____
_____
_____
_____
_____
_____
_____
_____
_____
_____
_____

Shrimp Pasta Salad

Shrimp, raw, peeled and deveined
Paprika
Olive Oil
Cheese Tortellini, cooked, prepared and cooled
Garlic, minced

Basil Pesto
Salt & Pepper
Pine Nuts
Oregano
Cherry Tomatoes, halved

Heat Olive Oil in a sauté pan. Lightly sauté Shrimp until just cooked and pink. Chill. In a bowl, toss Tortellini, Pesto, Pine Nuts, Shrimp, Cherry Tomatoes. Mix well.

Notes/Journal:

_____
_____
_____
_____
_____
_____
_____
_____
_____
_____
_____
_____
_____
_____

Table of Contents- Chapter 2

Swedish Meatballs 24
Beef Enchiladas 25
Shepherd's Pie 26

Mandarin Orange Chicken Salad 27
BBQ Chicken Meatballs 28
Taco Turkey Meatloaf 29

Shrimp Alfredo 30
Asian Sesame Salmon 31
Sea Salt and Cracked Pepper Salmon 32

Pork Tenderloin with Cranberries 33
Maple glazed Pork Tenderloin Medallions 34
Spaghetti with Italian Sausage 35

Gourmet Mushroom and Swiss Frittata 36
Smoked Salmon Quiche 37
Fried Rice with Egg and Pork 38

Spaghetti Pie 39
Macaroni and Cheese with Peas 40
Snow Pea Stir Fry 41

White Bean and Spinach Soup 42
Spicy Lentil Soup 43
Italian Sausage Salad 44

Auntie Lissa's Quick Menu Facts- Chapter 2

Aged Parmesan
AKA: Parmigiano Reggiano, aged about 2 + years, hard, and complex in flavor.

Leek Maintenance
Rinse Leeks well. Chop off rough green tops and bottom roots. Slice into rings and place in cold Water. Clay and dirt granules will drop to the bottom of the bowl. Sauté in Butter.

Many Mushrooms
White Mushrooms, Cremini, Portabella, Shiitake, Oyster, Enoki Chanterelle, Porcini, Shimeji, Morel

Pancetta v. Prosciutto
Pancetta comes from the belly of the pig and is cured. Prosciutto comes from the hind leg and is salt cured and air dried.

Temperatures
Fish: 145 degrees F
Poultry: 165 degrees F
Pork: 145 F and Pulled: 205 F
Beef: Rare- 125 F Well- 160F

Fresh v. Dried Herbs
1 T Fresh = 1 t Dried.
Dried are more potent and concentrated.

Hard Boiled Eggs
Place Eggs in a pot and add cold Water 1 inch over Eggs. Bring to a boil. Boil for 10 minutes. Remove from heat and run under cold water until cold.

Basic Vinaigrette
In food processor or blender:
¾ c Olive Oil, ¼ c Vinegar, Salt & Pepper, Herbs and Seasonings.

Scrambled Eggs
Beat Eggs and Salt & Pepper in medium bowl. Heat Butter in a skillet until hot. Pour in Eggs. As Eggs begin to set, pull spatula through the Eggs. Cook and pull until firm and fluffy (do not overcook).

Spinach Stats
High in nutrients and low in calories. Great source of iron. Spinach helps with diabetes management and lowers blood pressure.

Taco Seasoning
1 T Chili Powder, 1 t Cumin, 1 t Garlic Powder, 1 t Paprika, ½ t Oregano, ½ t Onion Powder, ¼ t Red Pepper Flakes, Salt & Pepper.

Panko v. Breadcrumbs
Panko is made from crustless White Bread that is coarsely ground. Breadcrumbs may be made with any type of Bread.

Roux
4 T Pan Drippings or Butter and 6 T Flour. Heat Fat (Dripping/Butter). Add Flour and whisk.

Green Onions v. Scallions
Same/Same!

Swedish Meatballs

Meatballs:
Ground Beef
Parsley
Nutmeg
Salt & Pepper
Panko
Olive Oil

Ground Pork
Allspice
Yellow Onions, grated
Garlic, minced
Eggs

Gravy:
½ c Butter
4 c Beef Stock
¼ t Allspice
1 c Heavy Cream

1 1/2 c Flour
Salt & Pepper
¼ t Nutmeg

Meatballs:
    Mix all ingredients and roll into balls. Heat oil in a sauté pan and cook meatballs.

Gravy:
    Make roux with Butter and Flour. Add Stock a little at a time. Whisk in Salt & Pepper, Allspice, and Nutmeg. Slowly add Heavy Cream. Bring Gravy up in heat. Add Meatballs. Serve warm.

Notes/Journal:

_____
_____
_____
_____
_____
_____
_____
_____

Beef Enchiladas

Olive Oil
Enchilada Sauce
Onion, diced
Green Bell Pepper, diced
Can Diced Tomatoes

Sour Cream
Black Beans, rinsed and drained
Cheddar Cheese, shredded
Tortillas
Ground Beef

Preheat the oven to 350 degrees F.
Heat Olive Oil in a sauté pan. Sauté Onions and Peppers.
Add Beef and brown. To pan, add the Tomatoes, Beans, Salt & Pepper, and a tablespoon of Enchilada Sauce. Bring up to heat.
Add Sour Cream then remove the pan from the burner. Mix.
Put some Enchilada Sauce in the bottom of a baking dish. Place a scoop of Beef mixture in a Tortilla and add Cheddar Cheese. Roll Tortilla and place in the dish. Repeat until the baking dish is full of rolled Tortillas.
Pour remaining Enchilada Sauce over Tortillas and top with Cheese.
Bake the dish of Enchiladas for 30 minutes in the oven.

Notes/Journal:
A spicier choice: Substitute any spicier Chili or Pepper with the Green Bell Pepper.

_____
_____
_____
_____
_____
_____
_____
_____
_____

Shepherd's Pie

Ground Beef
Onions, diced
Carrots, diced
Celery, diced
Peas
Corn
Garlic, minced
Salt & Pepper

Thyme
Beef Stock
Cornstarch Slurry
Russet Potatoes, large dice
Butter
Sour Cream
Chives, sliced
Cheddar Cheese, shredded

Preheat the oven to 350 degrees F.
Heat the Oil in a sauté pan. Sauté Onion, Carrots, and Celery. Add Beef and brown. When Beef is browned add the Garlic, Thyme, and Stock. Bring Stock up to a boil. Add Peas and Corn. Adjust flavors with Salt & Pepper. Tighten the liquid with Cornstarch Slurry. In a separate pot, boil heavily salted Water and boil the Potatoes. When the Potatoes are soft, prepare them into mashed Potatoes for the topping. Add Butter, Sour Cream, and Chives to the Potatoes.
Pour Beef Gravy and Vegetables into a baking dish. Top with mashed Potatoes. Evenly cover Beef Gravy and Vegetables with Potatoes. Top dish
with shredded Cheddar Cheese.
Bake in a preheated oven for 30 minutes.

Notes/Journal:

    Other Meat choices may include ground Lamb, ground Turkey, or ground Venison.

_____

_____

_____

_____

_____

_____

_____

_____

Mandarin Orange Chicken Salad

Chicken Breast, roasted and diced
Mandarin Oranges, drained and loosely chopped, set aside juice
Celery, chopped

Mayonnaise
Almonds, sliced
Salt & Pepper

Mix all ingredients in a large bowl. If dressing/salad is too tight, then thin with Mandarin Orange Juice until desired consistency. Chill and serve over Mixed Greens, on a Roll, or by itself.

Notes/Journal:

Mandarin Orange Cocktails:
Mandarin Orange Lemon Drop Cocktail- Whatever Mandarin Orange Juice is not used in the Salad, make a tasty Cocktail using 1.5 ounces of Vodka, .5-ounce Triple Sec, .75 ounce of Lemon Juice, and 1-ounce Mandarin Orange Juice.
Mandarin Martini- ⅓ c Mandarin Orange Juice, 2 ounces of Vodka, and 1 ounce Orange Liqueur.

_____
_____
_____
_____
_____
_____
_____
_____
_____
_____
_____

BBQ Chicken Meatballs

Ground Chicken
Breadcrumbs
Egg
Garlic, minced

Olive Oil
Salt & Pepper
Parsley
BBQ Sauce

Preheat the oven to 350 degrees F.
Heat Olive Oil in a sauté pan. Combine all ingredients except BBQ Sauce in a mixing bowl. Form into balls. Brown Meatballs in hot Oil.
Remove from heat. Drizzle Meatballs with BBQ Sauce. Place the pan into the oven and bake until Meatballs are to temperature.

Notes/Journal:

BBQ Sauce:
 1 ½ c Brown Sugar
 ½ c Red Wine Vinegar
 1 T Worcestershire Sauce
 2 t Paprika
 Dash of Tabasco

 1 ½ c Ketchup
 ½ c Water
 2 ½ T Dry Mustard
 Salt & Pepper

_____
_____
_____
_____
_____
_____
_____
_____
_____
_____

Taco Turkey Meatloaf

Ground Turkey
Egg
Breadcrumbs
Onion, finely diced

Taco Seasoning
Red Bell Pepper, finely diced
Taco or Picante Sauce

Preheat Oven in 350 degrees, F.
Mix all ingredients together. Cover and refrigerate 1 hour to meld flavors. Shape into loaf. Refrigerate again, if desired. Place into a lightly greased loaf pan. Top with a light layer of Taco Sauce.
Bake in the oven for 30-40 minutes

Notes/Journal:

Taco Seasoning:
1 T Chili Powder
1 t Garlic Powder
½ t Oregano
¼ t Red Pepper Flakes
1 t Cumin
1 t Paprika
½ t Onion Powder
Salt & Pepper

_____
_____
_____
_____
_____
_____
_____
_____
_____
_____

Shrimp Alfredo

Linguine Pasta, cooked and drained
Shrimp, lightly cooked to just pink
Butter
Garlic, minced

Salt & Pepper
Flour
Heavy Cream
Parmesan Cheese, grated

Melt Butter in a heated sauté pan. Add Garlic. Cook Garlic until fragrant. Add Flour and make Roux. Whisking slowly, add Cream until Sauce forms. Add Salt & Pepper to taste. Stir in and melt Parmesan.
Place Pasta on a platter. Fold Shrimp into Alfredo Sauce. Drizzle Sauce and place Shrimp over Pasta to serve.

Notes/Journal:

Try adding wilted Spinach to the Alfredo Sauce.

_____
_____
_____
_____

Asian Sesame Salmon

Salmon Portions   Soy Sauce
Salt & Pepper   Sesame Seeds
Sesame Oil

Heat Sesame Oil in a sauté pan. Season Salmon with Salt & Pepper. Sear top of Salmon in a hot pan. Flip Portion over. Splash Soy Sauce on top of Salmon and sprinkle with Sesame Seeds. Finish Fish in a hot oven.
Bake until just cooked.
Remove Salmon from the pan and serve.

Notes/Journal:

_____
_____
_____
_____
_____
_____
_____

Sea Salt and Cracked Pepper Salmon

Salmon Portions
Coarse Sea Salt
Fresh Cracked Indian Tellicherry Peppercorns

Olive Oil
Lemon, wedges

Heat Olive Oil in a sauté pan. Place Lemon wedges in the hot pan. Season Salmon with Salt & Pepper. When Lemon wedges are soft place Salmon top side down and sear. Flip Portion and cook until finished. Squeeze Lemon over portions and discard.
Remove from pan and serve.

Notes/Journal:

_____

_____

_____

_____

_____

_____

_____

_____

Pork Tenderloin with Cranberries

Pork Tenderloin
Red Wine
Cranberries, dried

Shallot, finely sliced
Garlic, minced
Salt & Pepper

Preheat the oven to 350 degrees F.
Season Pork with Salt & Pepper. Heat Olive Oil in a sauté pan. Sauté Shallots and Garlic until fragrant and soft. Add more Olive Oil and heat to very hot. Do not burn Shallots and Garlic. Sear all sides of Pork Loin. Keep Shallot and Garlic moving so it does not burn. Add Cranberries.
Do a quick stir to combine Shallot, Garlic, and Cranberries.
Deglaze pan with Red Wine and reduce. Place the entire pan in the heated oven and finish off Pork. Pork needs to be an internal temperature of 145 degrees, at least. Remove Pork from the pan after resting. Cut into medallions, place on plate/platter.
Finish plate by spooning Cranberry Sauce on pieces.

Notes/Journal:
I had a client request Cherries over the Cranberries. The process is the same however the flavor is on the sweeter side.

_____

_____

_____

_____

Maple glazed Pork Tenderloin

Pork Tenderloin   Salt & Pepper
Maple Syrup   Olive Oil

Preheat the oven to 350 degrees F.
Season Pork with Salt & Pepper. Heat Olive Oil in a sauté pan. Sear all sides of Pork Loin. Pour Maple Syrup over Pork. As Maple Syrup runs off Loin, baste Pork continuously until Syrup starts to reduce. Place the entire pan in a heated oven. Bake Pork until it reaches a minimum temperature of 145 degrees. Remove Pork from the pan after resting.
Cut into medallions and place on a plate/platter. Finish the plate by spooning reduced Syrup over Pork.

Notes/Journal:

_____
_____
_____
_____
_____
_____

Spaghetti with Italian Sausage

Ground Bulk Italian Sausage OR
Italian Sausage Links
Olive Oil
Onion, diced
Green Bell Pepper, diced
Garlic, Minced
Can Diced Tomatoes

Can Tomato Sauce
Spaghetti Pasta, cooked and drained
Salt & Pepper
Oregano
Basil
Thyme
Red Pepper Flakes

Heat Olive Oil in a sauté pan. Add Onions and Green Pepper, sauté until soft.
If using Ground Italian Sausage, add and brown.
Add Garlic and Seasonings to Meat mixture. Combine. Add Tomato Sauce and Diced Tomatoes. Bring up to a boil. Reduce heat and simmer.
If using Sausage Links, heat and brown in a separate pan. Add to Sauce.
Plate the cooked Pasta and top with Sauce.

Notes/Journal:
Try adding sliced Mushrooms, shredded Carrots, or Red Onion.

_____
_____
_____
_____
_____
_____
_____
_____
_____
_____

Gourmet Mushroom and Swiss Frittata

Cremini Mushrooms, sliced
Shiitake Mushrooms, sliced
Oyster Mushrooms, sliced
Baby Portabella, sliced
Green Onion, sliced

Swiss Cheese, shredded
Garlic, minced
Sage
Salt & Pepper
Butter

Heat the oven to 350 degrees F.
Heat and melt Butter in a sauté pan. Sauté Green Onions and Mushrooms. Drain extra liquid. Add Salt & Pepper, Garlic, and Sage. Drain again, if needed.
Place Butter in a baking dish and melt in the oven. Add Mushroom mixture and bake for 5 minutes. In a separate bowl, whisk Eggs. Add Cheese to the baking dish and pour Eggs over Mushrooms and Swiss.
Bake in the oven for 30-40 minutes. Bake until Egg is firm. Cool slightly before cutting. Serve.

Notes/Journal:

Smoked Salmon Quiche

Pie Crust
Leeks, cleaned and sautéed in Butter
Smoked Salmon, sliced
Eggs

Dill
Garlic, minced
Parmesan, grated
Heavy Cream

Preheat the oven 350 degrees F.
Place Leeks in Pie Crust followed by the Parmesan and Smoked Salmon. Season with Dill, Salt & Pepper. Whisk together the Eggs and Cream. Pour the mixture over the Fish and the Leeks.
Bake in the oven 30-40 minutes or until set and firm.

Notes/Journal:

_____
_____
_____
_____
_____
_____
_____
_____
_____
_____
_____
_____
_____

Fried Rice with Egg and Pork

Rice, prepared
Soy Sauce
Sesame Oil
Ground Pork, browned
Eggs, lightly scrambled

Peas
Carrots, diced
Broccoli, trimmed florets
Green Onion, sliced
Garlic, minced

Heat Sesame Oil in a sauté pan. Brown Pork. Transfer Pork to a bowl.
Scramble Eggs in Sesame Oil and Soy Sauce. Add and sauté Vegetables and Garlic.
Toss Pork, Vegetables and Rice together.
Heat all and serve.

Notes/Journal:

There are lots of choices for Vegetables in this dish. Try shredded Zucchini, diced Mushrooms, or thinly sliced Bok Choy.

_____
_____
_____
_____
_____
_____
_____
_____
_____
_____
_____

Spaghetti Pie

Spaghetti Pasta, cooked and drained
Eggs
Parmesan, grated
Onion, diced
Green Bell Pepper, diced
Garlic, minced

Italian Seasoning
Salt & Pepper
Can Diced Tomatoes
Can Tomato Sauce
Mozzarella, shredded

Preheat the oven to 350 degrees F.
Heat Olive Oil in a sauté pan. Sauté Onion, Green Bell Pepper and Garlic. Add Tomato Products, Italian Seasoning, Salt & Pepper. Bring to a quick boil then remove from heat. Stir in Pasta and let mixture completely cool. In a separate bowl, whisk the Egg and stir in ½ each of the Cheeses. Fold together the Pasta and Egg Mixtures. Pour into a lightly greased pie plate. Press slightly.
Top with remaining cheese.
Bake for 30 minutes or until Pie is hot and Cheese is melted.

Notes/Journal:

Homemade Mac N Cheese with Peas

Flour
Butter
Heavy Cream

Macaroni Pasta, cooked and drained
Cheddar Cheese, shredded
Peas

In a hot pan make Roux with Flour and Butter.
Slowly whisk in Cream and add Cheddar.
When Cheddar is melted and Sauce is at desired consistency, add Pasta and Peas.
Toss well and serve

Notes/Journal:

Optional Method: Place Mac n Cheese with Peas in baking or casserole dish. Mix melted Butter with Breadcrumbs or Panko. Top Mac n Cheese with Crumb topping and bake in a 350 degrees F oven until topping is golden.

_____
_____
_____
_____
_____
_____
_____
_____
_____
_____
_____
_____

Snow Pea Stir Fry

Snow Peas, rinsed well
Sesame Oil
Garlic, minced
Soy Sauce

Sesame Seeds
Brown Sugar/Honey
Rice, cooked

Whisk together Soy Sauce, Brown Sugar/Honey, and Garlic. Set aside.
Heat Sesame Oil in a wok or sauté pan. Start with firmer Vegetables and add one at a time to a hot pan. Stir fry about 1 minute each. When all desired vegetables are cooked, pour sauce over Vegetables and heat.
To serve, plate Rice and spoon Vegetables over.
Sprinkle Sesame Seeds on top. Serve.

Notes/Journal:

Optional Vegetables:
Green Onions, sliced
Green/Red/Yellow/Orange Bell Peppers
Bok Choy, chopped
Broccoli Florets
Carrots, sliced or diced
Mushrooms, sliced
Eggplant
Thai Eggplant
Napa Cabbage, sliced
Celery
White Radish
Watermelon Radish
Sugar Snap Peas

Optional Ingredients:
Tuxedo Sesame Seeds
Black Sesame Seeds
Pineapple, diced
Ginger, sliced or minced
Bamboo Shoots
Water Chestnuts
Fresh or Canned Bean Sprouts
Red Pepper Flakes
Peanut Oil
Lemon Grass

_____

_____

_____

_____

_____

_____

White Bean and Spinach Soup

Olive Oil	Stock
Onion, diced	Basil, stemmed and ribboned
Carrots, diced	Salt & Pepper
Celery, diced	Spinach, roughly chopped
Garlic, minced	Can White Beans, OR Pink
Can Diced Tomatoes	Beans, OR Cannellini, OR Great Northern, OR Garbanzo Beans

Heat Olive Oil in a sauce pot or stock pot. Sauté Onion, Carrots, Celery until tender. Add Garlic and mix. Stir in Basil, Diced Tomatoes, Stock, Beans, Salt & Pepper. Bring up to a boil. Reduce heat and add Spinach.
Simmer until flavors come together and meld

Notes/Journal:

Serve with homemade Bread.

In a bread machine:

½ c Milk	1 T dried or 3 T fresh Rosemary
¼ c Vegetable Broth	¼ t Sage
¼ c Olive Oil	1 t Salt
2 c Unbleached All-purpose Flour	1 ½ t Active Dry Yeast

_____

_____

_____

Spicy Lentil Soup

Olive Oil
Carrots, small dice
Onion, small dice
Celery, small dice
Garlic, minced
Stock
Lentils
Can Diced Tomatoes

Chili Powder
Ground Cumin
Garlic Powder
Paprika
Oregano
Sea Salt
Ground Pepper
Crushed Red Pepper Flakes

Heat Olive Oil in a stock pot. Add Carrots, Celery, and Onion. Sauté until tender. Add Garlic and toss quickly.
Add a few tablespoons of Stock and Diced Tomatoes to the Vegetables. Stir and pull up the heat. Add Herbs and Seasonings. Mix well. Stir in Lentils and heat.
Add remaining Stock just above the Lentils. Bring Soup to a boil.
Cook until Lentils are split and tender however not mushy. This is a Soup not a side dish. So make sure you have sufficient Stock.

Notes/Journal:
Garnish with Sour Cream, Green Onion, Chives, Mexican Blend shredded Cheese.

_____
_____
_____
_____
_____
_____
_____
_____
_____
_____

Italian Salad with Sausage

I

Romaine Lettuce, chopped
Roma Tomatoes, large dice
Kalamata Olives
Pepperoncini, whole
Italian Sausage Links, cooked, cooled and sliced

In large serving bowl, toss the Lettuce, Tomato, Olives, Peppers, Sausage, and Vinaigrette.

Vinaigrette:
Garlic, minced
White Wine Vinegar
Dijon Mustard
Mayonnaise
Honey
Worcestershire
Tabasco
Canola Oil
Salt & Pepper

In food processor, puree Garlic, Vinegar, Dijon Mustard, Mayonnaise, Honey, Worcestershire, Tabasco. Slowly add Canola Oil. Season with Salt & Pepper.

II

Rotini Pasta, cooked, drained, and cooled
Cherry Tomatoes, halved
Kalamata Olives
Broccoli, florets
Carrots, shredded
Italian Sausage Links, cooked, cooled and sliced
Pepperoncini, sliced

In large serving bowl, toss Pasta, Tomatoes, Olives, Broccoli, Carrots, Sausage, Pepperoncini, and Vinaigrette.

Notes/Journal:

_____
_____
_____
_____
_____
_____

Table of Contents - Chapter 3

Beef and Broccoli Stir Fry 47
Pasta Bolognese 48
Taco Casserole 49

Mediterranean Chicken Thighs 50
BBQ Turkey Meatballs 51
Chicken Wings 52

Cod Loin 53
Macaroni and Cheese with Tuna 54
Thai Chili Salmon 55

Rigatoni with Sausage, Dijon and White Wine Sauce 56
American Thick Pork Chops 57
Pork Medallions with Tomatoes, Prosciutto, and Arugula 58

Curry Egg Salad with Cucumber 59
Egg Drop Soup with Peas 60
Bacon and Shallot Quiche 61

Tri-Color Bell Pepper and Mushroom Rigatoni 62
Black Beans and Quinoa Bowl 63
Wild Rice stuffed Bell Peppers 64

Black Bean and Sweet Potato Chili 65
Garden Vegetable Soup 66
Caesar Salad 67

Auntie Lissa's Quick Menu Facts- Chapter 3

Cornstarch Slurry
Mixture of cold water with a thickening Cornstarch agent.
2 parts Water + 1 part Cornstarch

Verb: Baste
Pour juices or melted fat over food during cooking in order to keep it moist.

Jamaican Seasoning
Salt & Pepper, 1 T Garlic Powder,
2 t Cayenne, 1 T Onion Powder,
1 t Thyme, 1 T Parsley, 1 T Sugar,
2 t Paprika, ½ t Red Pepper Flakes,
½ t Nutmeg, ½ t Cumin. ½ t Cinnamon

What is Tarragon?
Tarragon is a grass-like herb with French and Russian varieties. Taste of Licorice and slight Vanilla. Used mainly in Fish dishes and Dressings.

Pineapple in a pinch
Pineapple is best with skin and core removed. I have found Pineapple with a yellowish skin is juicy.

Pepperoncinis
Sweet and mild chili pepper usually sold pickled. Tuscan Pepper, Sweet Italian Pepper, Golden Greek Pepper.

Swiss Chard Stats
35 calories/serving. 300% daily value vitamin K. Good source of vitamin A and C, magnesium, potassium, and fiber.

Turnips v. Parsnips
Both are Root Vegetables.
Parsnips are like Carrots = Sweet.
Turnips are like Radishes = Peppery and a little bitter.

Perfect Peppercorn
Pink, Green, Tellicherry Black, Malabar Black, Sarawak White, and Muntok White

Miso Paste
Traditional Japanese seasoning.
Fermented Soy Beans with Salt and Koji.

Frozen v. Fresh Vegetables
Frozen is a close second when consuming Vegetables. Fresh is always a first in taste and nutrition.

Pepper Steak Warning
Pepper Steak means with Bell Peppers not Ground Peppercorns.

Lemongrass Learning
Remove tough outer leaves. Cut off bulbs. Slice. Pulse in food processor.

Garlic Powder v. Garlic Salt
Powder is a mellow version of fresh. Garlic Salt is a Garlic flavored Salt. On the other hand, Onion Salt = Onion Powder + Salt

Beef and Broccoli Stir Fry

Cornstarch, divided
Flank Steak, thinly sliced
Soy Sauce
Brown Sugar
Garlic, minced

Ginger, minced
Broccoli, florets
Onion, sliced
Olive Oil
Rice, prepared

In a bowl, whisk together 2 T Cornstarch and 3 T Water. Add Steak to bowl and toss. In a separate bowl, whisk together 1 T Cornstarch, Brown Sugar, Soy Sauce, Garlic, Ginger, Salt & Pepper.
Heat Oil in a sauté pan. Add Beef to the pan and sear slices. Remove the Beef from the pan. Add Oil to pan juices. Add Broccoli and Onion. Cook until Broccoli is tender but not wilted. Add Beef back to the pan. Pour prepared Sauce over Beef and Vegetables. Bring Sauce up to a boil until it thickens. Serve over Rice.

Notes/Journal:
I love adding a very little bit of greens to this dish such as Bok Choy or Swiss Chard. My daughter likes to add a can of Bamboo Shoots and Sesame Seeds to this one.

_____

_____

Beef Bolognese

Olive Oil
Carrots, diced
Onion, diced
Celery, diced
Ground Beef
Garlic, minced
Oregano
Crushed Tomatoes
Bay Leaf

Pasta, cooked and drained
Basil, stemmed and ribboned or dried
Half and Half
Parmesan, grated
Pancetta, ribboned
Salt & Pepper
White Wine
Stock

Heavy Oil in a heavy saucepan. Add Onions, Carrots, Celery, Bay Leaf and Pancetta. Cook until Vegetables are soft and remove from the pan.
Add more Oil to the pan and heat. Add Beef and brown. Return Vegetables to the pan and add Garlic. Cook until fragrant. Add Wine and reduce until almost completely evaporated.
Stir in Tomatoes, Stock, and Oregano. Season with Salt & Pepper. Bring to a boil. Partially cover with a lid, reduce heat and simmer.
Remove and discard Bay Leaf and add Half and Half. Stir Sauce.
Serve over Pasta and top with Parmesan.

Notes/Journal:

Heavy Cream is a good substitute for Half and Half.

Taco Casserole

Olive Oil	Paprika
Ground Beef	Oregano
Salsa	Salt & Pepper
Onion, small dice	Red Pepper Flakes
Chili Powder	Corn, canned and drained or frozen
Cumin	Cheddar Cheese, shredded
Garlic Powder	Cornbread Batter, prepared

Preheat the oven 400 degrees F.
Heat Oil in a sauté pan. Sauté Onion until soft. Add Beef and brown. Season Beef with Herbs and Spices.
Add Salsa and Corn. Mix and heat. Transfer mixture to baking dish. Top with Cheddar Cheese and then cover completely with Cornbread Batter. Bake for 15 minutes. Pull the dish out of the oven. Pierce Bread with holes. Return Casserole to the oven. Continue baking for 15 minutes.
Cool slightly before serving.

Notes/Journal:

You can really play with the spiciness of this dish by choosing different Salsa heats.

_____

_____

Mediterranean Chicken Thighs

Chicken Thighs, skin on and bone in
Garlic, minced
Olive Oil
Lemon, thinly sliced
Kalamata Olives

Can Diced Tomatoes
Cumin
Paprika
Salt & Pepper

Heat oven to 350 degrees F.
Season individual Chicken Thighs with Garlic, Cumin, Paprika, Salt & Pepper.
Heat sauté pan to very HOT with Oil. Carefully place Chicken Thighs top side down in Oil.
Sear to crisp and flip. Carefully, pour Can of Tomatoes over Thighs. Add Olives and place Lemon Slices on Chicken.
Place the pan in the oven and bake until Chicken comes to temperature.
When serving, spoon Drippings, Tomatoes, and Olives over Thighs.

Notes/Journal:

_____
_____
_____
_____
_____
_____

BBQ Turkey Meatballs

Ground Turkey
Breadcrumbs OR
Panko
Egg
Italian Seasoning

Onion, finely diced
Salt & Pepper
BBQ Sauce
Olive Oil

Heat oven to 350 degrees F.
Heat Olive Oil in a sauté pan. Combine all ingredients except BBQ Sauce. Form mixture into balls. Brown Meatballs in a hot pan. Remove pan from heat and smother Meatballs with BBQ Sauce. Place Pan in the oven and bake until Turkey Meatballs are cooked through and BBQ is glazed and sticky.
Remove Meatballs from the pan. Place the pan back on the burner. Stir juices and BBQ Sauce together. Heat and reduce Sauce.
Serve Sauce over Meatballs.

Notes/Journal:

BBQ Sauce:
1 ½ c Brown Sugar
½ c Red Wine Vinegar
1 T Worcestershire Sauce
2 t Paprika

Dash of Tabasco
1 ½ c Ketchup
½ c Water
2 ½ T Dry Mustard
Salt & Pepper

Chicken Wings

Chicken Wings
Olive Oil
Salt & Pepper

Chili Bacon Maple-
Maple Syrup
Crushed Chili Pasta
Bacon, cooked and chopped

Maple Sriracha-
Cayenne
Ginger
Maple Syrup
Sriracha

Orange Ginger-
Garlic
Hoisin Sauce
Orange Juice
Ginger, grated
Soy Sauce

Other Sauces-
Maple Whiskey BBQ
Chipotle Aioli
Honey Garlic
Teriyaki
BBQ Sauce/ BBQ Rub
Buffalo
Lemon Pepper
Kung Pao

Preheat the oven to 400 degrees F.
Place seasoned and oiled Wings on a baking sheet and brush with choice Sauce. Bake until Wings are cooked through. Coat again with Sauce, if desired.

Notes/Journal:

Cod Loin

Cod Loin
Lemon, wedged
Basil, stemmed and ribboned or dried

Butter
Salt & Pepper

Heat oven to 350 degrees F.
In a sauté pan melt Butter. Add Lemon wedges to the pan and increase heat.
Carefully set Loin in pan and brush with Butter. Season Fish with Basil, Salt & Pepper.
Place the pan in the oven and bake until just done. DO NOT OVER BAKE!
Remove Fish from pan. Squeeze Lemon on Cod and serve.

Notes/Journal:

_____
_____
_____
_____
_____
_____
_____
_____
_____
_____
_____
_____
_____
_____

Macaroni and Cheese with Tuna

Flour and Butter for Roux
Heavy Cream
Cheddar, shredded

Salt & Pepper
Macaroni Pasta, cooked and drained
Can Tuna, drained

Slowly whisk Heavy Cream into hot Roux.
Add Cheddar Cheese a bit at a time while whisking. When Sauce is to desired consistency, add Pasta, drained Tuna, Salt & Pepper.
Toss well and serve.

Notes/Journal:

_____
_____
_____
_____
_____
_____
_____
_____
_____
_____
_____
_____
_____
_____
_____
_____

Thai Chili Salmon

Salmon Portions	Garlic, minced
Sesame Oil	Chili Garlic Sauce
Salt & Pepper	Bird's Eye Chili, dried and split

Heat oven 350 degrees F.
Heat Sesame Oil in a sauté pan. Salt & Pepper Salmon Portions. Smother Fish with Chili Garlic Sauce. Carefully, place Portion top side down in a heated pan. Sear quickly then flip.
Add Garlic and Bird's Eye Chili to Pan. Infuse the Oil.
Place the pan in the oven and bake Salmon until just done. Serve.

Notes/Journal:
Garnish Salmon with Bird's Eye Chili.

_____

_____

_____

_____

Rigatoni with Sausage and Dijon White Wine Sauce

Rigatoni, cooked and drained
Olive Oil
Hot Italian Sausage, ground bulk OR
Sausage Link, skin removed
White Wine

Heavy Cream
Dijon Mustard
Red Pepper Flakes
Basil, stems removed and ribboned, or dried

Heat Olive Oil in a large deep pan. Add Sausage Meat and brown.
Add the Wine and simmer, scraping the bits. Reduce Wine by half. Add Cream, Dijon Mustard, and Red Pepper Flakes to the pan and simmer.
Remove pan from burner. Toss in Pasta and Basil.
Serve.

Notes/Journal:

_____
_____
_____
_____
_____
_____
_____

American Thick Pork Loin Chops

Pork Loin Chops, 1 + inch thick, bone-in
Olive Oil
Brown Sugar
Paprika
Black Pepper

Salt
Chili Powder
Garlic Powder
Onion Powder
Cayenne

Heat grill.
Stir together all the Herbs and Spices including Brown Sugar in a small bowl. Season Pork Chop generously with the Seasoning Mix. Douse with Olive Oil. Place Chop on grill for a few minutes, give it a quarter turn clockwise to imprint diamond grill marks. Flip Pork Chop over and repeat.
Grill until Pork reaches temperature. Serve.

Notes/Journal:
Grilling on a Pellet grill really sharpens the flavors.

_____
_____
_____
_____
_____

Pork Medallions with Tomatoes, Prosciutto and Arugula

Olive Oil
Prosciutto, thinly sliced
Garlic, minced
Pork Tenderloin, cut crosswise, 1-inch Medallions

Salt & Pepper
Balsamic Vinegar
Arugula, stems removed and chopped
Plum Tomatoes, diced

Heat Oil in a sauté pan. Add Prosciutto and Garlic. Stir until Garlic is fragrant and golden. Transfer ingredients.
Season Pork Medallions. In a very HOT pan, sear each side. Transfer Pork.
Deglaze pan with Balsamic Vinegar include bits. Reduce Vinegar by more than half.
Place Arugula in bunches in pan and wilt. Add Tomatoes and Prosciutto, then toss. Season with Salt & Pepper.
Place Pork Medallions on plate or platter and spoon Sauce mixture over Pork pieces.

Notes/Journal:

_____
_____
_____
_____
_____
_____
_____
_____
_____
_____
_____
_____

Curry Egg Salad

Eggs, hard boiled, cooled and chopped
Celery, sliced
Green Onion, chopped

Curry
Mayonnaise
Cucumber, diced

In a mixing bowl, combine all ingredients.
Refrigerate and serve chilled.

Notes/Journal:
There are many types of Curry Powders. You can really play with the heat.

_____
_____
_____
_____
_____
_____
_____
_____
_____
_____
_____
_____
_____
_____
_____

Egg Drop Soup

Egg
Chicken Stock
Cornstarch
Ginger, minced
Soy Sauce

Scallions, sliced
Peas, canned and drained or frozen
Carrots, diced
Salt & Pepper
Shiitake Mushrooms, stemmed and sliced

Lightly whisk Egg in small bowl.
Pour some Stock into a separate bowl and add Cornstarch to make a Slurry.
Pour remaining Stock into stock pot. Add Ginger, Soy Sauce, Scallions, Peas, Carrots, Mushrooms, Salt & Pepper. Stir.
Bring Soup up to a boil. Slowly add Cornstarch Slurry whisking constantly. Drizzle whisked Egg into Soup, making cooked Egg ribbons.
Remove from heat. Add Salt & Pepper to taste.

Notes/Journal:

_____
_____
_____
_____
_____
_____
_____
_____
_____
_____
_____
_____

Bacon and Shallot Quiche

Pie Crust
Bacon, cooked and crumbled
Heavy Cream
Egg

Salt & Pepper
Shallot, sliced and sautéed with Garlic
Pepper Jack Cheese, shredded
Red Pepper Flakes

Heat oven to 350 degrees F.
In a mixing bowl, whisk together Heavy Cream, Egg, Salt & Pepper, and Red Pepper Flakes. In Pie Crust place the Cheese, Bacon, Shallots, and Garlic. Pour in Egg Mixture. Bake for 30 minutes or until Egg us set and firm. Cool slightly before cutting into wedges to serve.

Notes/Journal:

_____
_____
_____
_____
_____
_____
_____
_____
_____
_____
_____
_____
_____

Tri-Color Bell Pepper and Mushroom Rigatoni

Rigatoni, cooked and drained
Onion, diced
Green Bell Pepper, diced
Red Bell Pepper, diced
Yellow/Orange Bell Pepper, diced
Garlic, minced
Can Diced Tomatoes
Can Tomato Sauce

Cremini Mushrooms, sliced
Shiitake Mushrooms, sliced
Oyster Mushrooms, sliced
Baby Portabella, sliced
Basil, stemmed and ribboned or dried
Parmesan, grated
Olive Oil

Heat Olive Oil in a large pan. Add Onions and sauté until almost translucent. Add Bell Peppers and Garlic. Sauté. Add Mushrooms in the order of most firm to tender. Sauté and drain accumulated liquid if needed.
Slowly pour Diced Tomatoes and Tomato Sauce over Vegetables. Mix well. Bring up to a boil and add Basil. Reduce and simmer.
Remove Sauce from heat and toss with the cooked Pasta. Top with Parmesan and serve immediately.

Notes/Journal:
Toss Mozzarella Pearl Balls into Sauce and Pasta for a different meal. Serve with Garlic Bread and Red Wine. For an appetizer create a Charcuterie Board:

    Prosciutto
    Goat Cheese
    Figs
    Olives
    Pickled Peppers

Black Bean Quinoa Bowl

Quinoa
Roma Tomatoes, small dice
Avocado, diced and splashed with Lime Juice to prevent browning
Can Black Beans, rinsed and drained
Can Corn, drained
Bell Pepper, diced
Jalapeno, diced

Dressing:
¼ c Olive Oil
1 ½ T Lime Juice
1 t Sugar
1 t Cumin
½ T Garlic, minced
½ T Red Wine Vinegar
Salt & Pepper

Whisk together dressing and refrigerate.
Toss together the Quinoa and Vegetables.
Fold in the Dressing. Toss well and serve.

Notes/Journal:

_____
_____
_____
_____
_____
_____
_____
_____

Wild Rice Stuffed Bell Peppers

Red Bell Peppers, cut in half from top to bottom; seeded and ribs removed
Tomato Sauce
Can Diced Tomatoes
Onion, small diced
Green Bell Pepper, small diced

Oregano
Parsley
Red Pepper Flakes
Salt & Pepper
Wild Rice, prepared
Cheddar Cheese, shredded
Mushrooms, chopped

Heat oven to 350 degrees F. Place Bell Pepper halves in the oven to par-bake.
In a bowl, stir together the remaining ingredients, reserving ¼ c of Tomato Sauce and ¼ c Cheddar Cheese.
Stuff the Pepper halves with filling. In a baking dish pour remaining ¼ c Tomato Sauce. Place filled Peppers in the baking dish. Top Red Bell Peppers with the remaining ¼ c Cheddar Cheese.
Bake until filling is heated through and Cheese is melted.

Notes/Journal:

Black Bean Sweet Potato Chili

Black Beans, rinsed and drained
Ground Beef
Olive Oil
Onion, diced
Poblano Pepper, ribs removed, seeded and diced

Salt & Pepper
Garlic, minced
Chipotle in Adobo, chopped or pureed
Sweet Potato, diced
Quinoa

Puree half the Black Beans in a food processor. Set mixture aside.
In a stock pot, add Onions and Poblano in hot Oil. Sauté until tender.
Brown the Ground Beef in the Onion and Pepper mixture. Season with Salt & Pepper. Add Garlic and Chipotle. Cook until fragrant and flavors meld.
Add Sweet Potato, pureed Black Beans, whole Black Beans, and Water. Bring Chili up to a boil. Stir in Quinoa. Continue cooking until Quinoa blooms and Sweet Potato softens.

Notes/Journal:
Garnish with Sour Cream.

_____
_____
_____
_____

Garden Vegetable Soup

Leeks, cleaned and rinsed
Carrots, diced
Celery, diced
Russet Potatoes, diced
Can Diced Tomatoes
Green Beans, 1 inch pieces

Corn, drained or frozen
Thyme
Salt & Pepper
Stock
Olive Oil

Heat Olive Oil in a stock pot. Sauté Leeks with Salt & Pepper and Thyme. Add Carrots and Celery, sauté until soft.
Next add Tomatoes, Potatoes, and Stock. Bring Liquid up to a boil. When Potatoes are soft and still firm, add the Corn and Green Beans.
Reduce to a simmer. Simmer until flavors meld.

Notes/Journal:

_____
_____
_____
_____
_____
_____
_____

Caesar Salad with Chicken

Romaine Lettuce, leaves separated, washed and dried
Parmesan Cheese, grated

Dressing:
2 Garlic Cloves, minced
1 t Anchovy Paste
2 T Lemon Juice
1 t Worcestershire Sauce

Croutons
Roasted Chicken Breast, cut on the diagonal- 2 inch strips

1 c Mayonnaise
½ c Parmesan, grated
Salt & Pepper

In a food processor, puree the Garlic, Anchovy Paste, Lemon Juice, Dijon Mustard, Worcestershire Sauce, Mayonnaise, Parmesan Cheese, Salt & Pepper. Chill.
In a large bowl, toss the Romaine and the Dressing. Place in a serving bowl or dish and top with Chicken Breast, Parmesan, and Croutons.

Notes/Journal:
Add Endive or Radicchio for color or flavor boost.

Table of Contents- Chapter 4

Beef Stew 70
Teriyaki Meatballs 71
Pepper Steak 72

Roasted Chicken Quarters 73
Turkey Shepherd's Pie 74
Chicken and Vegetable Enchiladas 75

Chili glazed Shrimp with Rice Noodles 76
Lime and Pineapple Salmon 77
Lemon Pepper Tilapia 78

Wisconsin Brats and Kraut 79
Sliced Ham with Pineapple and Cherries 80
Jamaican Pork Chops 81

Asparagus and Thyme Quiche 82
Smoked Salmon Egg Baguette 83
Bacon and Red Potato Frittata 84

Thai Coconut Curry 85
Cheesy Tortellini and Spinach Alfredo 86
Miso Ramen Bowl 87

Black Bean and Tortilla Soup 88
French Onion Soup 89
Crab Salad 90

Auntie Lissa's Quick Menu Facts- Chapter 4

Garbanzo Beans v. Chickpeas
Same/Same!!

Pasta Magic
Boil Salted water in a large pot. Add Pasta. Stir Pasta. Boil Pasta. Test Pasta. Drain Pasta. Enjoy Pasta.

Is Coconut Milk 'Milk'
Coconut Milk is dairy free, lactose free, vegan, and soy free. It is a 'milky' white liquid extracted from the grated pulp of a Coconut.

Dictionary:
Savory
1. (of food) belonging to the category that is salty or spicy rather than sweet.

Growing Greens
Alfalfa- Rinse 2 T's seeds. Place Seeds in quart jar. Add ¼-½ c cold water, cover with sprouting screen and soak overnight.

Quick Keto
Low carb, moderate protein, higher fat diet that can help some people burn fat effectively.

Feasting on Flowers- Friends or Foe
Warning some prep needed: Begonia, Chrysanthemum, Clover, Cornflower, Day Lily, Daisy. No No's: Delphinium, Oleander, Azalea, Calla Lily, Hyacinth. This list is very short. As always, do your research first.

Golden Raisins
Golden and Regular Raisins are made with the same type of Grape. Golden Raisins are dehydrated and Brown are dried in the sun.

Very Vidalia
Vidalia's are Sweet Onions but not all Sweet Onions are Vidalia. Grown in Vidalia, Georgia. A squat, egg-shaped Yellow Onion.

Frittata v. Quiche
Quiche is made with Ingredients, Eggs, and Heavy Cream (Milk or ½ and ½). Frittatas have no Crust and very little if any Milk or Cream.

Anchovy Pasta
Comes in toothpaste type tubes. Anchovy, Salt, and Olive Oil, ground into a greyish Paste.

Super San Marzano Tomatoes
Most popular Plum Tomato from Italy. Low in acidity, bright red, low seed count, and easy to remove skins.

Fabulous Flank
Flank Steak is a cut of Beef taken from the abdominal muscles or lower chest of a steer.

Beer Batter v. Tempura Batter
Beer Batter: Flour, Egg, and Beer.
Tempura: Flour, Egg, Water, Ice.

Beef Stew

Stew Beef, large dice
Red Potatoes, halved or quartered
Turnips, large dice
Parsnips, large dice
Carrots, baby or 1 inch slices
Celery, 1 inch slices

Onion, large dice
Beef Stock
Bay Leaves
Thyme
Salt & Pepper
Flour or Cornstarch Slurry

Stove Top:
Heat oil in a stock pot. Shake Beef in Flour. Brown Beef in hot Oil. Lower heat a bit and add Onion and sauté. Slowly add Stock and increase heat. Season the Stock with Herbs and Spices. Add Potatoes, Turnips, Parsnips, Carrots, and Celery.
If foregoing the Flour, pull stew temperature up to a boil and add the Slurry.

Crock Pot:
Place Beef, Potatoes, Turnips, Parsnips, Carrots, Celery, and Onion into crockpot. Stir in Stock, Thyme, and Bay Leaves, season with Salt & Pepper to taste. Cover and cook for 6 hours. In a small bowl, whisk together Flour and Stock. Stir Flour mixture into the crockpot. Cover and heat until thick.

Notes/Journal:
Always remove Bay Leaves before serving.

_____

_____

Teriyaki Meatballs

Ground Beef   Salt & Pepper
Ground Pork   Teriyaki Sauce
Egg   Sesame Oil
Breadcrumbs   Sesame Seeds

Preheat the oven to 350 degrees F.
In a mixing bowl combine Beef, Pork, Egg, Breadcrumbs, Salt & Pepper, Garlic, a tablespoon of Teriyaki, and a teaspoon of Sesame Seeds. Roll Into balls.
Heat Sesame Oil in a sauté pan. When hot, brown the Meatballs. Remove from heat. Brush Meatballs with Teriyaki. Place the pan in a preheated oven. Baste with Teriyaki throughout baking. Bake until Meatballs are cooked through and Teriyaki has glazed. Sprinkle with additional Sesame Seeds before serving.

Notes/Journal:

Beef/Pork Ratio's: ½ Beef + ½ Pork or ¾ Beef + ¼ Pork.

Teriyaki Sauce:
1 c Water	--	
¼ c Soy Sauce	--	
5 t Brown Sugar	--	Cook in a saucepan until heated.
1 T Honey	--	
½ t Ground Ginger	--	
¼ t Garlic Powder	--	
2 T Cornstarch	>	Mix and add to the saucepan.
¼ c Water	>	Cook and stir until thick.

Pepper Steak

Soy Sauce
Rice Wine Vinegar
Brown Sugar
Cornstarch
Vegetable Oil
Salt & Pepper
Rice, prepared

Flank Steak, thinly sliced against the grain
Green Bell Pepper, ribbed and seeded, julienne
Red Bell Pepper, ribbed and seeded, julienne
Onions, sliced
Garlic, minced
Ginger, minced

Sauce: Whisk ¼ c Soy Sauce, 1 T Vinegar, 1 ½ T Sugar, 1 ½ T Cornstarch, 3 T Water.
Heat Oil in a sauté pan. Season Steak with Salt & Pepper then sear on all sides. Remove from the pan.
Add more Oil to the pan and heat. Sauté Peppers and Onions. Add Garlic and Ginger. Cook until fragrant and flavors meld. Slide Vegetables to the side. Pour in Sauce and whisk or stir until thick. Return Beef to the pan. Mix well. Serve over Rice.

Notes/Journal:
Some recipes call for a wedged Tomato added just after the sauce thickens. Eh, I could go either way with that.

_____
_____
_____
_____

Roasted Chicken Quarters

Whole Raw Chicken Quarters, bone in, skin on
Butter, softened not melted
Thyme, fresh and trimmed or dried
Rosemary, fresh and trimmed or dried
Garlic, minced
Salt & Pepper

Preheat the oven to 400 degrees F.
Place rack on sheet tray. Place Chicken pieces on a rack, evenly spaced.
Cut Butter into pats. Rub or smash Butter pieces under the skin and on top of the skin. Make sure the Chicken pieces are completely covered.
Grind Salt & Pepper over Chicken. Follow with the Garlic, Thyme, and Rosemary. Rub Herbs gently into the skin.
Bake Chicken 40 minutes to 1 hour until Chicken is cooked to temperature and the skin is brown and crispy. Throughout baking, baste the pieces with the melted pan Butter and drippings.

Notes/Journal:
Skin on- Bone in: Thighs, Legs, Any part of the Chicken will do.

Turkey Shepherd's Pie

Ground Turkey
Onions, diced
Carrots, diced
Celery, diced
Peas
Corn
Garlic, minced

Salt & Pepper
Rosemary
Stock
Cornstarch Slurry
Russet Potatoes, large dice
Butter
Sour Cream

Preheat the oven to 350 degrees F.
Heat Oil in a sauté pan. Sauté Onions, Celery, and Carrots. Add Ground Turkey and brown.
Add Garlic, Rosemary and Stock.

** Pause** Consider this: Use fresh Rosemary Sprigs. Infuse the Sprigs into the Hot Oil prior to sautéing the Vegetables and browning the Turkey. Remove the Sprigs before placing finished gravy into the baking dish.

Bring Stock up to a boil. Add Peas and Corn. Adjust the flavor with Salt & Pepper. Tighten the liquid with Cornstarch Slurry. In a separate pot, prepare Mashed Potatoes with Potatoes, Salt & Pepper, Butter and Sour Cream.
Pour Turkey mixture and Vegetables into a baking dish. Top evenly with Mashed Potatoes.
Bake in a preheated oven for 30 minutes or until Gravy is bubbly.

Notes/Journal:

_____
_____
_____
_____
_____
_____
_____

Chicken and Vegetable Enchilada

Zucchini, peeled and small dice
Green Onion, sliced
Cilantro
Garlic, minced
Cheddar Cheese, shredded
Corn, drained

Tortillas
Enchilada Sauce
Black Beans, rinsed and drained
Green Chilis
Olive Oil
Chicken, roasted and shredded

Preheat the oven to 350 degrees F.
Heat Oil in a sauté pan. Sauté Zucchini, Green Onions, and Garlic. Reduce heat and stir in Cilantro, Corn, Beans, Green Chilis, Chicken and a few tablespoons of Enchilada Sauce.
In a lightly greased baking dish, spoon a tablespoon of Enchilada Sauce into the bottom of the baking dish. Stuff and roll the Tortillas with the Chicken mixture filling and place in the pan.
Repeat until a complete single layer of rolls line the pan.
Pour remaining Enchilada Sauce onto rolls and top with Cheddar Cheese.
Bake the Enchilada for 30 minutes or until filling is heated and Sauce is bubbling.

Notes/Journal:
Make ahead and freeze or split between multiple baking dishes.

_____
_____
_____
_____
_____
_____
_____
_____
_____
_____
_____
_____
_____

Chili glazed Shrimp with Rice Noodles

Shrimp, peeled and deveined
Salt & Pepper
Oil
Garlic
Rice Noodles, prepared

Sauce:
   Thai Sweet Chili Sauce
   Chili Garlic Sauce
   Lime
   Sugar

Whisk or pulse in a food processor the Sauce ingredients together and chill.
Heat Oil in a sauté pan. Quickly sear Shrimp on both sides with Garlic. Remove Shrimp from the pan. Do Not Burn Garlic.
Lower heat and add Sauce. Heat until slightly reduced and thickened. Add Shrimp.
Finish cooking Shrimp in Sauce. Place cooked Shrimp on Rice Noodles. Pour Sauce over Shrimp and Noodles.

Notes/Journal:
There are many types of Rice style or Ramen style Noodles that can be used. I've used Green Tea Noodles and Squid Ink Noodles for this dish.

Lime and Pineapple Salmon

Salmon Portions
Salt & Pepper
Lime, wedged
Pineapple, cored, skinned, diced or canned
Pineapple Juice

Brown Sugar
Olive Oil
Various Stir Fry Vegetables
Lime Juice

Preheat the oven to 350 degrees F.
In a baking dish place Salmon Portions. Season Portions with Salt & Pepper. Dust Salmon heavily with Brown Sugar. Drizzle Lime Juice and Pineapple Juice over Salmon Portions. Place the dish in the oven and bake until Fish is 'just' done.
Meanwhile heat Oil in a sauté pan. Stir fry Pineapple chunks and wedges of Lime until warm.
Add and sauté the Various Stir Fry Vegetables of your choosing.
Remove Salmon from the oven. Place Portions on a plate to the side.
Pour Salmon drippings over Pineapple (Vegetables) and Lime. Squeeze Lime wedges over Pineapple. Make a sauce with the Liquids. Add Water if needed.
Remove and discard Lime wedges.
Plate up Salmon with the Pineapple (and Vegetables).
Pour Sauce over Salmon.

Notes/Journal:

Stir Fry Vegetable Ideas:

Baby Corn	Bamboo Shoots	Water Chestnuts
Broccoli	Bok Choy	Watermelon Radish
Shredded Carrots	Bell Pepper	Green Onion
Mushrooms	Sugar Snap Peas	Asparagus
Sprouts	Zucchini	Cabbage

_____
_____
_____
_____
_____
_____
_____

Lemon Pepper Tilapia

Tilapia Portions
Butter
Fresh Ground Tellicherry Peppercorns

Lemon Juice
Lemon, wedged
White Wine

Melt Butter in a hot pan. Add Lemon wedges to Butter. Add White Wine. Turn up heat and reduce Wine by half or more.
Place Peppercorn seasoned Tilapia top side down into the pan. Add Lemon Juice or Water for desired taste. Flip Portion in pan and finish. Squeeze wedges into pan. Remove and discard Lemon peel.
Serve with Pan Juices over fish.

Notes/Journal:
Tellicherry Peppercorns are a larger Peppercorn and make up a small percentage of the Peppercorn crop.

Wisconsin Brats and Kraut

Bratwurst Links
Kaiser Rolls
Beer, cheap
Sauerkraut

Onions, sliced
Butter/Olive Oil
Dijon Mustard
Ketchup

Preheat a grill.
In a large pot place Brats, Onions, and Beer. Boil until Brats are almost cooked through.
Remove Brats from liquid and place on the grill.
Remove Onion slices and reserve but discard liquid.
In a separate pan, heat Sauerkraut. Slice Kaiser Rolls and toast on the grill. Place flat pan or sauté pan on grill. Add Oil and Onions. Caramelize Onions.
To Serve: Apply Dijon and Ketchup to Roll.
Place Brat on top.
Add Onions and Kraut.

Notes/Journal:

Quick Potato Salad
5 Potatoes, boiled, peeled, cooled, and chopped
3 Eggs, hard boiled, peeled, cooled, and chopped
½ c Onion, diced

½ c Celery, diced
½ c Sweet Pickle Relish ¼ t Garlic Salt
¼ t Celery Salt
1 T Yellow Mustard
Black Pepper
¼ c + Mayonnaise

_____
_____
_____
_____
_____
_____
_____
_____

Sliced Ham with Pineapple and Cherries

Baked Ham, sliced
Brown Sugar
Pineapple, cored, peeled, and sliced
Pineapple Juice
Maraschino Cherries

Preheat the oven to 350 degrees F.
Place Ham Slice in a baking dish. Lightly sprinkle Brown Sugar over Ham. Sprinkle the second layer of Brown Sugar and drizzle Pineapple Juice over.
Bake just until Ham is heated and Brown Sugar has melted into a glaze.
Serve.

Place Pineapple slice on top with Cherry in the center.

Notes/Journal:

Jamaican Pork Chops

American Cut Pork Chops, sliced 1 inch
Olive Oil
Salt & Pepper
Garlic Powder
Cayenne
Allspice
Thyme

Parsley
Sugar
Paprika
Onion Powder
Red Pepper Flakes
Nutmeg
Cinnamon

Preheat the grill.
Mix Salt & Pepper, Garlic Powder, Cayenne, Onion Powder, Thyme, Parsley, Sugar, Paprika, Red Pepper Flakes, Nutmeg, and Cinnamon.
Season Chops heavily with Jamaican spice mixture and splash with Olive Oil. Marinate several hours or overnight. Place Chop on grill for a few minutes, give it a quarter turn clockwise to imprint diamond grill marks. Flip Chop over and repeat.
Grill until Pork reaches temperature. Serve.

Notes/Journal:

Seasoning:
Salt & Pepper
2 t Cayenne
1 t Thyme
1 T Sugar
2 t Paprika
½ t Nutmeg

1 T Garlic Powder
1 T Onion Powder
1 T Parsley
½ t Cinnamon
½ t Red Pepper Flakes
½ t Cumin

_____
_____
_____
_____
_____
_____
_____
_____

Asparagus and Thyme Cheesy Quiche

Pie Crust
Asparagus, slice ¼ inch, sautéed with
Garlic
Cherry Tomatoes, halved, optional
Heavy Cream

Salt & Pepper
Thyme, fresh, stems removed or dried
Parmesan, shredded
Eggs

Preheat the oven to 350 degrees F.
In a mixing bowl, whisk together Heavy Cream, Eggs, Salt & Pepper. Place Asparagus, Thyme, Parmesan, and Cherry Tomatoes in Pie Crust. Pour Egg mixture into Crust and over Vegetables. Bake in a preheated oven 30-40 minutes until the center is set and firm. Cool slightly before cutting into wedges and serving.

Notes/Journal:

_____
_____
_____
_____
_____
_____

Smoked Salmon and Egg Baguette

Sourdough Baguette, V cut at the top and removed, create a 'boat'
Swiss Cheese, shredded
Smoked Salmon, sliced
Eggs

Sour Cream
Salt & Pepper
Scallions, thinly sliced
Capers, drained
Fresh Chives, chopped

Preheat the oven to 350 degrees F.
Place Baguette on a parchment paper lined sheet tray. Lay Cheese, Salmon slices, and Scallions in the 'boat'. Whisk together Egg, Sour Cream, Chives, Salt & Pepper. Pour into Bread over the Cheese and Salmon.
Bake for 20 minutes or until Egg us firm and set.

Notes/Journal:

_____
_____
_____
_____
_____
_____
_____
_____
_____
_____
_____
_____
_____
_____

Bacon and Red Potato Frittata

Butter
Red Potatoes, thinly sliced
Fresh Basil, loosely chopped and stems removed
Salt & Pepper

Garlic, minced
Green Onions, thinly sliced
Bacon, cooked crisp
Parmesan, grated
Eggs

Preheat the oven to 350 degrees F.
Place Butter in a baking dish in the heated oven. When Butter is melted, pull the pan out of the oven and place Red Potatoes in a single layer. Salt & Pepper the Potatoes. Bake until Potatoes are soft. Add another tablespoon of Butter in the pan and melt in the oven. Add Green Onion to the pan and bake until soft. Add Bacon, Basil, and Garlic to the pan. Top with Parmesan. Whisk Eggs, Salt & Pepper. Pour Eggs over Potatoes and Cheese.
Bake for 30-40 minutes or until Frittata is firm and set. Cool slightly before cutting and serving.

Notes/Journal:

Thai Coconut Curry

Red Bell Pepper, 2 inch julienne
Yellow/Orange Bell Pepper, 2 inch julienne
Green Onion, sliced
Basil Leaves, stems removed
Pea Pods
Carrots, thinly sliced on the diagonal

Lime, wedged
Coconut Milk
Curry Paste
Ginger, thinly sliced
Olive Oil
Red Pepper Flakes, optional

Heat Oil in sauté pan or wok. Sauté Bell Peppers, Green Onion, and Carrots. Squeeze Lime wedges and then add to pan.
Pour Coconut Milk over Vegetables and pull up the heat. Add Curry Paste, Basil, Ginger, and Red Pepper Flakes. Mix and stir. Add Pea Pods.
Cook until Vegetables are tender, and Sauce thickens slightly.
Remove and discard Lime wedges.
Serve over Rice.

Notes/Journal:

_____
_____
_____
_____
_____

Tortellini and Spinach Alfredo

Cheese Tortellini, cooked and drained
Spinach
Butter

Heavy Cream
Salt & Pepper
Parmesan, grated

In a pan, heat the Butter and Cream. Season with Salt & Pepper. Add Parmesan and whisk until melted. Stir in Spinach and wilt.
Serve Alfredo over Tortellini OR Toss Tortellini with Sauce.

Notes/Journal:

Miso Ramen Bowl

Olive Oil
Garlic, minced
Ginger, minced
Bean Sprouts, rinsed
Cabbage, thinly sliced
Carrots, shredded or small julienne
Stock

Sugar
Soy Sauce
Miso Paste
Sesame Oil
Chukamen Chinese or Japanese style Ramen Noodles, prepared

Start heating up a pan and add Oil. To the heating Oil add the Garlic and Ginger. Add Bean Sprouts, Cabbage, and Carrots. Sauté until Vegetables are tender.
Add Stock, Sugar, and Soy Sauce. Bring up heat to a boil. Reduce heat and dissolve Miso Paste in Stock. Add a splash or shake of Sesame Oil.
Remove from heat. Ladle Soup over Vegetables and serve.

Notes/Journal:

Black Bean and Tortilla Soup

Olive Oil
Onion, diced
Bell Pepper, diced
Carrots, diced or shredded
Lime, wedged
Black Beans, rinsed and drained
Tortillas

Stock
Diced Tomatoes
Corn
Jalapeno, seeded and diced
Garlic, minced
Salt & Pepper
Taco Seasoning

Heat oven to 375 degrees F.
In pot sauté Onion, Bell Pepper, Carrots, Jalapeno, and Lime wedges in Oil. Add Garlic, Salt & Pepper.
In a separate bowl, mix Taco Seasonings.
Add Stock, Tomatoes, Corn, and Seasonings to pot. Bring to a boil then reduce to a simmer.
Cut Tortillas into strips. Brush Tortilla strips with Olive Oil. Arrange in a single layer on a sheet tray. Bake, flip, bake.
Stir Tortilla strips into Soup right before serving.

Notes/Journal:

Taco Seasoning:
Chili Powder
Onion Powder
Red Pepper Flakes

Oregano
Paprika
Cumin

_____
_____
_____
_____
_____
_____
_____
_____
_____

French Onion Soup

Yellow Onions, several- sliced
Olive Oil
Stock
Bay Leaves
Thyme
Salt & Pepper

Butter
Cabernet
Flour
Provolone, sliced
Sourdough Bread, sliced

Heat Olive Oil in a stock pot. Add Onions and Thyme. Sauté Onions on lower heat. Let cook until translucent. Salt & Pepper the Onions and add Butter. Increase heat. Add Wine and deglaze the pan. Add Flour and Bay Leaf. Add Stock.
Bring Soup back up to a boil then back down to a simmer.
Toast Sourdough Bread with Olive Oil in the oven.
Remove and discard the Bay Leaf.
Ladle Soup into soup bowl. Top with toasted Sourdough. Place a slice of Provolone on Bread. Broil in the oven until Cheese is melted and begins to brown.
Serve.

Notes/Journal:

_____
_____
_____
_____
_____
_____
_____
_____
_____
_____
_____
_____

Crab Salad

Jumbo Lump Crab Meat
Celery, small dice
Tarragon, stemmed and chopped finely or dried
Chives, finely chopped or dried

Mayonnaise
Sour Cream
Lemon Juice
Dijon Mustard
Salt & Pepper

In a bowl, toss Crab, Celery, Tarragon, and Chives.
In a separate bowl, stir/whisk Mayonnaise, Sour Cream, Lemon Juice, and Dijon Mustard.
Fold together Dressing and Crab mixture. Season with Salt & Pepper.
Chill.

Notes/Journal:

Serve On/In:
Cucumber
Tomato
Crostini

Toast
Lettuce Wrap
Rolls

_____
_____
_____
_____
_____
_____

Table of Contents - Chapter 5

Spaghetti and Meatballs ……………………………………………………… 93
Stuffed Bell Peppers ………………………………………………………….. 94
Italian Beef with Portobello and Vidalia Onions ……………………………. 95

Turkey Pot Pie …………………………………………………………………. 96
Sweet and Sour Chicken ……………………………………………………… 98
Curry Chicken Salad ………………………………………………………….. 99

Shrimp with White Wine Butter Sauce ……………………………………….100
Salmon Cakes with Lemongrass ……………………………………………..101
Salmon with Swiss Chard, Corn, and Cherry Tomatoes ……………………102

Pork Patties with Cajun Coleslaw …………………………………………….103
Pork Tenderloin with Lemon and Fennel …………………………………….104
Pork Roast ……………………………………………………………………..105

Mini Vegetable Egg Cups ……………………………………………………..106
Broccoli and Bell Pepper Quiche ……………………………………………..107
Cheesy Red Potato Frittata …………………………………………………..108

Chickpea Curry ………………………………………………………………..109
Mediterranean stuffed Zucchini with Kefir and Mint ………………………..110
Soba with Miso glazed Eggplant ……………………………………………..111

10 Bean Chili …………………………………………………………………..112
Navy Bean and Ham Soup ……………………………………………………113
Tuna Salad in Tomato Cup ……………………………………………………114

Auntie Lissa's Quick Menu Facts- Chapter 5

Curry Paste
Paste made with Coriander Seed, Cumin, Black Peppercorns, Red Bell Pepper, Red Chilies, Lemongrass, Ginger, Garlic, Turmeric, Sea Salt, Lemon Juice, Lime, Green Onions, Avocado Oil, Coconut Sugar.

Easy Starch: Mashed Potatoes
Bring a pot of Salted Water to a boil.
Add large diced Potatoes. Cook/ boil Potatoes until soft through.
Add Butter, Salt, or Sour Cream and Mash/Whip until smooth.

Roasting Right
Potatoes, Carrots, Sweet Potato, Parsnips, Onions, Brussel Sprouts
Toss well in Olive Oil, place on parchment lined sheet tray.
Roast in a very hot oven.

Water Chestnuts
It's not a nut but a Vegetable that is grown under water, in the mud.

Popular Pickling Spices
Mustard Seeds, Allspice Berries, Coriander Seeds and Red Pepper.
You can Pickle: Asparagus, Beets, Bell Peppers, Cauliflower, Carrots, Fennel, Onions……

Great Grills
Gas, Charcoal, Pellet, Propane, Natural Gas.
Popular Brands: Weber, Blackstone, Traeger, Char Broil, Napoleon, Green Egg.

Wild Caught v. Farm Raised
Wild caught is caught from a natural habitat.
Farmed Seafood is raised in tanks.

Really Rice
Bring 2 c of Water with 1 c Rice to a boil.
Cover.
Reduce to a simmer.
Simmer for 10 minutes or until Rice is soft.

Bay Scallops v. Sea Scallops
Sea Scallops are very large. 3 x's larger.
Bay Scallops are sweeter and more tender.
Bay are only found on the East Coast in bays and harbors.

Silver Skin
A thin membrane of connective tissue found on various meats.

Herbs de Provence
Thyme, Basil, Rosemary, Tarragon, Savory, Marjoram, Oregano, and Bay Leaf.
Great for Vegetables, Chicken, Grilled Fish, Tomato based Soups, and Stews.

Big Beef Burgers
Rare: 120-125
Medium Rare: 130-135
Medium: 140-145
Medium Well: 150-155
Well: 160-165

Spaghetti and Meatballs

Pasta Sauce:
- Onions, diced
- Green Bell Pepper, diced
- Garlic, minced
- Can Diced Tomatoes
- Can Tomato Sauce
- Basil, stemmed and chopped or dried
- Salt & Pepper
- Olive Oil

Meatballs:
- Ground Beef
- Ground Pork
- Garlic, minced
- Egg
- Breadcrumbs
- Italian Seasoning
- Salt & Pepper

Pasta

Sauce: Sauté Onion, Green Pepper, and Garlic in Oil. Add Basil, Tomato Sauce and Diced Tomatoes. Season with Salt & Pepper. Simmer.
Meatballs: Mix all ingredients and season with Salt & Pepper. Roll Meat into balls. Heat Olive Oil in a pan and brown the Meatballs. Cook through and add Meatballs to Sauce.
Pasta: Follow manufacturer's directions on package to prepare Pasta.
Serve: Place Pasta in a dish or on a plate. Top with Sauce and Meatballs.

Notes/Journal:

You may prepare large batches of Sauce and freeze. Also, the longer the sauce simmers the tastier it will be. Some traditional recipes call for a tablespoon of Sugar.

_____
_____
_____
_____
_____
_____
_____
_____
_____
_____

Stuffed Bell Peppers

Bell Peppers, any type, sliced from top to bottom, ribbed and seeded
Ground Beef
Can Tomato Sauce
Can Diced Tomatoes
Onion, small dice
Green Bell Pepper, small dice

Mushrooms, small dice
Oregano
Parsley
Red Pepper Flakes
Salt & Pepper
Brown Rice, prepared
Cheddar Cheese, shredded

Preheat the oven to 350 degrees F. Place Bell Pepper halves in the oven to par-bake.
In a bowl, mix Ground Beef, 3/4 Tomato Sauce, Diced Tomatoes, Onion, Green Bell Pepper, Mushrooms, Oregano, Parsley, Red Pepper Flakes, Salt & Pepper, Brown Rice, and 1/2 Cheddar Cheese.
Remove halved Bell Peppers from the oven. Cool slightly. Stuff Peppers with Ground Beef mixture.
In a baking dish, pour remaining Tomato Sauce. Place stuffed Peppers in the dish. Top with remaining Cheddar Cheese.
Bake in the oven for 20 minutes, until Beef is cooked through and Cheese is melted.

Notes/Journal:
You can really get creative with Stuffed Peppers.

Instead of:
Whole Bell Pepper

Ground Beef
Diced Tomatoes
Brown Rice

Try:
Large Poblano, Red/Yellow/Orange Bell Pepper
Ground Turkey/Chicken/Venison
Chunky Salsa any temperature
White/Wild Rice, Quinoa, Farro

_____
_____
_____
_____
_____
_____
_____
_____

Italian Beef with Portobello and Vidalia Onions

Roast Beef, sliced
Au Jus or Beef Stock
Pepperoncinis
Pepperoncini Juice
Portobello Mushrooms, sliced
Vidalia Onions, halved once and sliced
Salt & Pepper

Basil, dried
Parsley, dried
Garlic Powder
Bay Leaf
Olive Oil
Kaiser Rolls, slit in side
Provolone, sliced (optional)

In a large stock pot, heat Oil. Sauté Onions until translucent. Add Mushrooms and sauté until soft. Pour Stock just over Vegetables. Add to Stock, Pepperoncini Juice, Salt & Pepper, Oregano, Basil, Parsley, Garlic Powder, and Bay Leaf. Bring liquid up to a boil. Reduce heat to a simmer. Add Beef and Pepperoncinis. Remove pot from burner, discard Bay Leaf.

With tongs place Beef and Vegetables in Roll. If desired top with Provolone.

Place Sandwich on a plate or dish. Serve with Au Jus in ramekin or a small dish on the side.

Notes/Journal:

Chicago Style:
  Sliced Beef Roast
    (roasted w/ Onion, Italian Seasoning, Red Pepper Flakes, Garlic, Red Wine, Beef Stock, Thyme)
  Green Bell Peppers
    (sautéed with Garlic, Kosher Salt, and Black Pepper)
  Giardiniera
  French Rolls

_____
_____
_____
_____
_____
_____
_____

Turkey Pot Pie

Pie Crust
Ground Turkey or Shredded
Carrots, diced
Celery, diced
Peas
Corn, frozen or canned and drained
Onion, diced

Stock
Thyme, stemmed and chopped or dried
Garlic, minced
Cornstarch Slurry
Salt & Pepper
Olive Oil

Preheat the oven to 350 degrees F.
Heat Oil in a shallow stock pot. Add Onions and cook with Thyme until translucent. Add Carrots, Celery, Garlic, Salt & Pepper. Sauté until Vegetables are soft. Add and brown Ground Turkey. Add Peas and Corn.
Cover Turkey and Vegetables with Stock. Bring up to a boil. Thicken soup into a gravy with the Cornstarch Slurry.
With a slotted spoon, spoon the Turkey and Vegetables into Pie Crust. When Turkey and Vegetable are level with the top, pour gravy over. Top with second Pie Crust. Trim and crimp edges. Bake in the oven for 25 minutes or until the crust browns.

Notes/Journal:

Pie Crust:
2 ½ c Flour
1 t Salt
6 T unsalted Butter
¾ c Vegetable Shortening
½ c Ice Water

Mix the Flour with the Salt. Add Butter and Shortening. 'Cut' into pea size bits. Make ice cold Water with the Water and Ice. Measure ½ c of Ice Water and add 1 T at a time to the Flour. Eventually when Dough forms, transfer to a Floured surface and fold. When ingredients are incorporated, form Dough into ball, then disks, and refrigerate. Roll out and place 1 crust in a pie dish, fill with gravy, place 2nd crust on top, and bake.

Sweet and Sour Chicken

Pineapple Chunks, fresh or canned
Snow Peas, rinsed and drained
Red Bell Pepper, seeds and ribs removed, large diced
Onion, large dice
Carrots, shredded
Broccoli Florets, trimmed
Chicken Breast, cooked and diced
Rice, prepared

Brown Sugar
Pineapple Juice
Cornstarch Slurry made with Cornstarch and Pineapple Juice
Soy Sauce
Ginger, minced
Sesame Oil
Sesame Seeds

Sauté Onion, Bell Pepper, and Carrots in Sesame Oil. Add Broccoli, Snow Peas, Pineapple, and Chicken.
In a separate bowl, whisk together Pineapple Juice, Garlic, Brown Sugar, Cornstarch, Ginger, and Soy Sauce. Pour Soy Sauce mixture over Chicken and Vegetable. Stir and heat.
Remove from heat when Sauce thickens and adheres to Chicken and Vegetables.
Serve over Rice.

Notes/Journal:
The red in Sweet and Sour Chicken Sauce is just red food coloring. There are a lot of good all-natural red food colorings out there. Annatto is an all-natural way to color food.

Curry Chicken Salad

Chicken Breast, cooked and diced or shredded
Salt & Pepper
Mayonnaise
Apples, peeled and diced

Curry Powder
Celery, sliced
Green Onion, sliced
Raisins, golden
Cashews, rough chopped

In a small bowl, mix Mayonnaise, Salt & Pepper, and Curry.
In a separate bowl, toss the Chicken, Apples, Celery, and Green Onion Fold dressing into mixture.
Toss Raisins and Cashews in Salad. Chill. Serve.

Notes/Journal:
Tart Apples are a great choice to this dish. This Salad is absolutely fabulous served as a Lettuce Wrap. As a very high protein dish, it keeps in the refrigerator for daily lunches or quick snacks.

Shrimp with White Wine Butter Sauce

Butter
Shallot, thinly sliced
Garlic, minced
Shrimp, raw, peeled, and deveined

Salt & Pepper
Stock
White Wine
Lemon, wedged

Heat Butter in a sauté pan. Add 2 Lemon wedges. Sauté Shallots and Garlic. Add Wine and deglaze pan. Reduce by half.
Season Shrimp with Salt & Pepper. Add Shrimp to pan. Remove and discard Lemon. Cook Shrimp to just barely pink.
Whisk in Stock. Serve Shrimp on plate or dish. Spoon Wine Butter Sauce over Shrimp, garnish with remaining Lemon wedges.

Notes/Journal:

If you have the budget, definitely splurge and substitute Scallops for Shrimp. When using Scallops, I have also substituted Rum for the White Wine.

Salmon Cakes with Lemongrass

Lemongrass, remove outer layer, finely chopped or pureed in a food processor
Ginger, peeled and finely chopped
Dill
Mayonnaise
Panko

Egg
Green Onion, finely chopped
Salmon, raw- ½ chopped and ½ finely chopped
Olive Oil
Salt & Pepper

In a bowl combine chopped Lemongrass, Ginger, Dill, Green Onion, Salt & Pepper and all the Salmon. Mix well. Add Egg, Mayonnaise and Panko. Combine.
Form patties with the mixture. Heat Olive Oil in a pan. Place Patties in the pan. Brown on each side and make sure the center is cooked through.
Serve.

Notes/Journal:
Salmon Cakes can be made without Lemongrass or Ginger.

_____
_____
_____
_____
_____
_____
_____
_____

Salmon with Swiss Chard, Corn, and Cherry Tomatoes

Rainbow Swiss Chard, sliced an ½ inch pieces, stalk and leaves
Corn, frozen or canned and drained
Cherry Tomatoes

Olive Oil
Salmon Portions
Salt & Pepper

Heat Olive Oil in a sauté pan. Sauté Swiss Chard and add Corn. Sauté until Chard is tender. Add Cherry Tomatoes. Sauté until Tomato skins wrinkle and almost split. Season with Salt & Pepper. Remove Vegetables from the pan.
Add more Oil to the pan and heat. Season Salmon Portions with Salt & Pepper. Place Salmon top down in a hot pan. Flip Salmon and finish to temperature.
Make a bed of Tomatoes and Chard on a plate or serving dish. Place Portion on Vegetables and serve.

Notes/Journal:

Pork Patties with Cajun Coleslaw

Patties:
Onion, grated
Breadcrumbs
Egg
Parsley
Ground Plain Pork
Salt & Pepper
Garlic Powder
Mayonnaise
Olive Oil

Coleslaw:
5 T Mayonnaise
2 T Yellow Mustard
2 T Olive Oil
1 t + Louisiana Hot Sauce
2 T Ketchup
1 T Red Wine Vinegar
1 T Worcestershire Sauce
1 Lemon, juiced
1 t Garlic Powder
Salt & Pepper
Onion, thinly sliced
Cabbage, thinly sliced or shredded

Patties:
Combine Onion and Parsley.
In a mixer or mixing bowl, combine Meat, Onion Mixture, Breadcrumbs, Egg, Salt & Pepper, Garlic Powder, and Mayonnaise. Shape mixture into patties.
Heat Olive Oil in a large sauté pan or flat top.
Place Patties and brown each side of the patty and cook through.

Coleslaw:
In a mixing bowl, whisk Mayonnaise and Mustard. Whisk in Oil until emulsified.
Whisk in Hot Sauce, Ketchup, Vinegar, Worcestershire, and Lemon Juice. Stir in Garlic Powder, Salt & Pepper. Chill Dressing. Dressing can also be emulsified in a blender or food processor. In a large mixing bowl toss together Onions and Cabbage. Pour Dressing over Vegetables and mix well.
Chill and Serve.

Notes/Journal:

_____

_____

_____

Pork Tenderloin with Lemon and Fennel

Pork Tenderloin
Fresh Rosemary
Salt & Pepper
Fennel Bulb, cleaned, halved and sliced
Artichoke Hearts, undrained

Kalamata Olives, pitted
Cherry Tomatoes
Lemon, wedged
Olive Oil

Preheat the oven to 400 degrees F.
Heat Oil in a sauté pan. Place Fresh Rosemary in the pan, stems and all. Infuse Oil with the Rosemary. Add the Lemon Wedges. Season Pork Tenderloin with Salt & Pepper. Turn up heat. Sear all sides of Tenderloin in the hot pan. Turn heat down and sauté Fennel until soft while Pork, Lemon, and Rosemary remain in the pan.
Add Artichoke Hearts with liquid, Kalamata Olives with about 2 tablespoons of liquid, and Cherry Tomatoes. Remove Rosemary stems but not the Lemon Wedges.
Place the pan in the oven and bake until Pork is to temperature. When up to temperature, take the pan out. Remove and discard Lemon Wedges and let Tenderloin rest on a cutting board.
Cut Pork into 1- 1 1/2-inch medallions. Place pieces on a dish or service plate. Spoon Fennel, Artichokes, Kalamata Olives, and Cherry Tomatoes over Medallions. Pour pan juices over Vegetables and Meat.
Serve.

Notes/Journal:

_____

_____

Pork Roast

Pork Roast
Garlic, minced
Salt & Pepper
Cornstarch
Stock
Red Potatoes, quartered

Balsamic Vinegar
Baby Carrots
Soy Sauce
Onion, large dice
Brown Sugar

In a bowl of crockpot or slow cooker, place Pork Roast. Salt & Pepper Roast. Whisk together Stock, Balsamic Vinegar, Soy Sauce, Garlic, and Brown Sugar.
Place Vegetables around Pork. Pour Stock mixture over Roast and Vegetables.
Roast in the crock pot for 6-8 hours.

For a Gravy:
In a liquid measuring cup, 1 cup or larger in size, ladle 1/4 c of liquid from the crock pot and add the Cornstarch. Whisk.
Add and whisk more liquid until it makes 1 full cup. Add to crockpot.

Notes/Journal:
A variety of Root Vegetables may be substituted: Parsnips or Turnips.

Mini Egg and Vegetable Cups

Onion, diced
Bell Peppers, seeded and ribs removed, diced
Mushrooms, diced
Basil, stemmed and ribboned or dried

Swiss Cheese, shredded
Garlic, minced
Salt & Pepper
Eggs
Olive Oil or Butter

Preheat the oven to 350 degrees F.
Grease muffin tin with Oil or Butter and set aside. Heat sauté pan and sauté Onion, Bell Pepper, and Mushrooms until soft. Salt & Pepper mixture. Add Basil and Garlic. Sauté a few minutes.
Whisk together Eggs and Salt & Pepper. Place a tablespoon or 2 of Vegetables into muffin cups. Top with Swiss Cheese and fill with Egg.
Bake for 15 minutes or until Egg is set and firm. Cool slightly on a rack. Serve warm.

Notes/Journal:

Broccoli and Bell Pepper Quiche

Pie Crust
Onion, small dice
Green Bell Pepper, small dice
Red Bell Pepper, small dice
Orange/Yellow Bell Pepper, small dice

Broccoli Florets, finely chopped
Pepper Jack Cheese, shredded
Heavy Cream
Eggs
Salt & Pepper

Preheat the oven to 350 degrees F.
Heat sauté pan with Oil. Sauté Onion and Bell Peppers until soft.
Whisk together Eggs, Heavy Cream, Salt & Pepper. Place Broccoli in the bottom of Pie Crust. Add 1/2 Swiss Cheese. Spoon Onion and Bell Pepper into Pie Crust. Top with remaining Cheese. Pour Egg and Heavy Cream in Crust.
Bake Quiche for 20 minutes or until Egg is set and firm. Cool slightly before cutting into wedges to serve.

Notes/Journal:
Jack Cheese is really good with the dish, however, Swiss Cheese is just as tasty.

Cheesy Red Potato Frittata

Butter
Red Potatoes, thinly sliced
Garlic Cloves, thinly sliced
Pepper Jack Cheese, shredded

Cheddar Cheese, shredded
Parmesan Cheese, shredded
Eggs

Preheat the oven to 350 degrees F.
Par-boil Potato slices until soft. Melt Butter. Pour 1 T of Butter into the bottom of a baking dish. Place 1 layer of Potatoes in the dish. Heat Oil in a sauté pan. Sauté Garlic slices until colored slightly. Place Garlic on a paper towel to drain off oil. Place 1 layer of Garlic slices on top of the Potatoes.
Whisk Eggs with Salt & Pepper. Layer the 1/2 the Cheese on top of the Garlic. Place the 2nd layer of Potatoes on Cheese followed by another layer of Garlic. Put remaining Cheese on Frittata. Fill the pan with the whisked Egg. Bake for 30 minutes or until Egg is firm and set. Cool slightly before slicing.

Notes/Journal:
Try Fingerling Potatoes instead of Red Potatoes.

Chickpea Curry

Olive Oil
Onion, sliced
Salt & Pepper
Curry Powder
Garlic, minced

Stock
Chickpeas, drained and rinsed (Garbanzo Beans)
Honey
Basmati Rice, prepared

Heat Oil in a sauté pan.
Add Onion and sauté until caramelized and brown. Season with Salt & Pepper. Stir in Garlic and Curry Powder. Add tablespoon of Stock and stir.
Add the Chickpeas, Coconut Milk, and Honey. Heat to a boil. Reduce heat and simmer.
Warm Rice and spoon Curry over.

Notes/Journal:
A pinch of Cayenne heats this dish nicely. Also, a pinch of Saffron gives it a lift.

Mediterranean Stuffed Zucchini with Kefir and Mint

Zucchini, halved lengthwise, slightly
hollowed out, topped with Olive
Oil and roasted
Olive Oil
Carrot, small diced
Green Bell Pepper, small dice
Red Bell Pepper, small dice
Orange/Yellow Bell Pepper, small dice
Cherry Tomatoes, quartered
Paprika
Red Pepper Flakes
Oregano
Salt & Pepper
Chives, chopped

Topping:
½ c Kefir
2 t Lemon Juice
⅓ c Mint Leaves, finely chopped
¼ Cucumber, finely chopped

Preheat the oven to 450 degrees F.
Heat sauté pan and add Olive Oil. Add Carrot, Peppers, Tomatoes, and hollowed part of Zucchini diced.
Season the Vegetables with Paprika, Red Pepper Flakes, Oregano, Salt & Pepper, and Chives.
Whisk the Kefir and Lemon Juice in a small separate bowl. Fold in Cucumber and Mint. Fill the Zucchini with the Vegetable Stuffing and roast until cooked and heated through.
Top the Zucchini and Vegetables with the Dressing. Serve.

Notes/Journal:
Dressing can be pureed in a food processor until smooth, if desired.

Soba with Miso-glazed Eggplant

Eggplant, sliced
Green Beans, snapped and cut in half on the diagonal
3 + T Sesame Oil
Soba Noodles, prepared, rinsed and drained
3 T Miso Paste
2 T Brown Sugar

2 T Red Wine Vinegar
1 T Soy Sauce
2 T Garlic, minced
2 t Ginger, minced
Baby Spinach, stemmed
Green Onion, sliced on the diagonal
Sesame Seeds

Salt and Oil the Eggplant. Place slices on the grill. Heat sauté pan and add Sesame Oil. Sauté Green Beans.
In a separate bowl, whisk together Miso Paste, Brown Sugar, Red Wine Vinegar, Soy Sauce, Garlic, Ginger, 3 T Sesame Oil and 2 T of Water.
Brush Eggplant with Dressing and return to the grill. Remove Eggplant from grill when heated through. Cut Eggplant into bite size pieces.
In a bowl, toss together Eggplant, Green Beans, Noodles, Spinach, Dressing, Onions, and Sesame.

Notes/Journal:

I like to purchase my noodles (Ramen, Rice, Soba, Green Tea) at the local Asian Market. There is always a huge variety. You can usually find some noodles at your grocery store however the selection is usually dismal and usually pricey. Utilizing the local Asian Market helps a local family.

Bean Chili

Black Beans
Red Beans
Kidney Beans
White Kidney Beans
Navy Beans
Great Northern Beans
Pinto Beans
Black Eyed Peas
Pink Beans

Small White Beans
Ground Beef
Onion, diced
Green Bell Pepper, diced
Can Diced Tomatoes
Can Tomato Paste
Stock
Chili Powder
Salt & Pepper

In a pot or stock pot heat Oil. Sauté Onions and Green Peppers. Brown Ground Beef. Add Diced Tomatoes and Stock. Season Stock with Chili Powder, Salt & Pepper. Add tender Beans to Soup. Adjust Stock level. Slightly thicken soup with Tomato Paste. Bring Soup up to a boil.
Reduce and simmer.

Notes/Journal:

If choosing canned Beans, this could turn out to be quite a large recipe in a huge stockpot. Chili can easily be frozen in family size containers. Bags of dried Beans labeled 10-Bean are available. Soak and sort Beans before making your pot of Chili. You can also purchase the individual type of dried Bean in a plastic sleeve. And NO, you do not need to use every single type of Bean to make this Chili. Whenever possible, I do like to add a can Garbanzo Beans.

_____

_____

Navy Bean and Ham Soup

Olive Oil
Can Diced Tomatoes
Garlic, minced
Onion, dice
Celery, dice
Carrots, dice

Ham, diced
Stock
Bay Leaf
Navy Beans, canned or dried
(sorted, soaked, and drained)

Heat Oil in a soup pot or stock pot. Sauté Onions, Celery, and Carrots until soft. Add Garlic, Bay Leaf, Salt & Pepper.
Pour in Diced Tomatoes, Ham, and tender Beans. Add Stock to the Soup and bring to a boil. Reduce and simmer until flavors meld. Remove and discard Bay Leaf before serving.

Notes/Journal:

Ham is super good in the recipe, however, try Bacon it really adds a smoky and salty flavor. Just remember to remove excess Bacon grease. It will form a film or extra layer of oil on the top of the Soup.

Tuna Salad in Tomato Cup

Can Tuna, drained
Celery, finely chopped
Red Onion, finely chopped
Parsley
Mayonnaise
Mustard
Salt & Pepper
Lemon Juice
Whole Fresh Tomato, washed, cored, and hollowed

  In a small mixing bowl, toss Tuna, Celery, Red Onion, Parsley, Salt & Pepper. In a separate bowl, whisk together Mayonnaise, Mustard, and Lemon Juice. Stir the 2 mixtures together.
Chill.
Spoon the Tuna Salad into each Tomato cup and serve.

Notes/Journal:
A way to transform this Salad is instead of Parsley try Dill OR Tarragon.

Index

10 Bean Chili .... Soup/Salad .... Ch 5
American Thick Pork Chops .... Pork ...... Ch 3
Asian Sesame Salmon .... Seafood .... Ch 2
Asparagus and Thyme Quiche .... Egg .... Ch 4

Bacon and Red Potato Frittata .... Egg .... Ch 4
Bacon and Shallot Quiche .... Egg .... Ch 3
Baked Ziti with Italian Sausage .... Pork .... Ch 1
Basil and Cherry Tomato Quiche .... Egg .... Ch 1
BBQ Chicken Meatballs .... Poultry .... Ch 2
BBQ Turkey Meatballs .... Poultry .... Ch 3
Beef and Broccoli Stir Fry .... Beef .... Ch 2
Beef Enchiladas .... Beef .... Ch 2
Beef Stew .... Beef .... Ch 4
Beef Stroganoff .... Beef .... Ch 1
Black Bean and Veg Enchiladas .... Vegetable .... Ch 1
Black Bean and Quinoa Bowl .... Vegetable.... Ch 3
Black Bean and Tortilla Soup .... Soup/Salad .... Ch 4
Broccoli and Bell Pepper Quiche .... Egg .... Ch 5

Cajun Red Beans and Rice .... Pork .... Ch 1
Caesar Salad .... Soup/Salad .... Ch 3
Cheese Tortellini Spinach Alfredo .... Vegetable.... Ch 4
Cheesy Red Potato Frittata .... Egg .... Ch 5
Chicken and Vegetable Enchiladas .... Poultry .... Ch 4
Chicken Wild Rice Soup ..... Soup/Salad ..... Ch 1
Chicken Wings ..... Poultry ..... Ch 3
Chickpea Curry ..... Vegetable .... Ch 5
Chili ..... Beef ..... Ch 1
Chili glazed Shrimp with Rice Noodles ..... Seafood ..... Ch 4
Citrus glazed Salmon ..... Seafood .....Ch 1
Crab Salad ..... Soup/Salad ..... Ch 4
Cod Loin ..... Seafood ..... Ch 3
Curry Chicken Salad ..... Poultry ..... Ch 5
Curry Egg Salad with Cucumber ..... Egg ..... Ch 3

Dill Salmon with Capers .... Seafood ..... Ch 1

Egg Drop Soup with Peas ...... Egg .... Ch 3
French Onion Soup ..... Soup/Salad ..... Ch 4
Fried Rice with Egg and Pork ..... Egg ..... Ch 2

Garden Vegetable Soup .... Soup/Salad ..... Ch 3
Gourmet Mushroom and Swiss Frittata ..... Egg ..... Ch 2

Ham and Pineapple and Cherry .... Pork ..... Ch 4

Italian Beef with Portobello and Vidalia Onions .... Beef ..... Ch 5
Italian Sausage Salad ..... Soup/Salad ..... Ch 2

Jamaican Pork Chops .... Pork ..... Ch 4

Leek and Potato Soup .... Soup/Salad ..... Ch 1
Lemon Pepper Tilapia ..... Seafood ..... Ch 4
Lime and Pineapple Salmon ..... Seafood ..... Ch 4

Macaroni and Cheese with Peas .... Vegetable .... Ch 2
Macaroni and Cheese with Tuna ..... Seafood ..... Ch 3
Mandarin Orange Chicken Salad ..... Poultry ..... Ch 2
Maple glazed Pork Tenderloin ..... Pork ..... Ch 2
Mediterranean Chicken Thighs ..... Poultry ..... Ch 3
Mediterranean stuffed Zucchini with Kefir and Mint ..... Vegetable .... Ch 5
Mini Vegetable Egg Cups ..... Egg ..... Ch 5
Mexican Meatloaf ..... Beef ..... Ch 1
Miso Ramen Bowl ..... Vegetable .... Ch 4

Navy Bean and Ham Soup .... Soup/Salad ...... Ch 5

Parmesan Chicken Meatballs .... Poultry ..... Ch 1
Pork with Tomatoes, Prosciutto and Arugula ..... Pork ..... Ch 3
Pork Patties with Cajun Coleslaw ..... Pork ..... Ch 5
Pork Roast ..... Pork ..... Ch 5
Pork Tenderloin with Apples ..... Pork ..... Ch 1
Pork Tenderloin with Cranberries .... Pork .... Ch 2
Pork Tenderloin with Lemon and Fennel ..... Pork ..... Ch 5
Pasta Bolognese ..... Beef ..... Ch 3
Pepper Steak ..... Beef ..... Ch 4
Potato Broccoli and Pepper Jack Egg Casserole ..... Egg ..... Ch 1

Quiche Lorraine .... Egg ..... Ch 1

Rigatoni with Sausage Dijon & White Wine .... Pork ..... Ch 3
Roasted Chicken Quarters ..... Poultry ..... Ch 4

Salmon Cakes with Lemon Grass .... Seafood ..... Ch 5
Salmon with Swiss Chard, Corn, Cherry Tomatoes ..... Seafood ..... Ch 5
Sea Salt and Pepper Salmon ..... Seafood ..... Ch 2
Shepherd's Pie ..... Beef ..... Ch 2
Shrimp Alfredo ..... Seafood ..... Ch 2
Shrimp Pasta Salad ..... Soup/Salad ..... Ch 1
Shrimp Scampi Pasta ..... Seafood ..... Ch 1

Shrimp with White Wine Butter Sauce ..... Seafood ..... Ch 5
Smoked Salmon Egg Baguette ..... Egg ..... Ch 4
Smoked Salmon Quiche ..... Egg ..... Ch 2
Snow Pea Stir Fry ..... Vegetable ..... Ch 2
Soba with Miso glazed Eggplant ..... Vegetable .... Ch 5
Spaghetti Pie ..... Vegetable .... Ch 2
Spaghetti and Meatballs ..... Beef ..... Ch 5
Spaghetti with Italian Sausage ..... Pork ..... Ch 2
Spicy Black Bean Chili ..... Soup/Salad ..... Ch 3
Spicy Lentil ..... Soup/Salad ..... Ch 2
Stuffed Bell Peppers ..... Beef ..... Ch 5
Swedish Meatballs ..... Beef ..... Ch 2
Sweet and Sour Chicken ..... Poultry ..... Ch 5

Taco Casserole .... Beef ..... Ch 3
Taco Turkey Meatloaf ..... Poultry ..... Ch 2
Teriyaki Meatballs ..... Beef ..... Ch 4
Thai Chili Salmon ..... Seafood ..... Ch 3
Thai Coconut Curry ..... Vegetable .... Ch 4
Tri-Color Bell Pepper and Mushroom Rigatoni ..... Veg ..... Ch 3
Tri-Color Bell Pepper Baked Ziti .... Vegetable .... Ch 1
Tuna Salad in Tomato Cup ..... Soup/Salad ..... Ch 5
Turkey Meatloaf ..... Poultry ..... Ch 1
Turkey Pot Pie ..... Poultry ..... Ch 5
Turkey Shepherd's Pie ..... Poultry .... Ch 4

Vegetable Enchiladas .... Vegetable .... Ch 1

Waldorf Chicken Salad .... Poultry ..... Ch 1
Wisconsin Brats and Kraut ..... Pork ..... Ch 4
Wild Rice stuffed Bell Peppers ..... Vegetable .... Ch 3
White Bean and Spinach Soup ..... Soup/Salad ..... Ch 2

About the Author

Chef Lissa Turner

Currently a Mom and Wife first.

In 1996, I discovered I could be a Chef and attended Culinary School right out of High School. During my early 20's, I enjoyed Golf Club Cuisine, Bar and Tavern Basics, Chain and Small Restaurant Kitchens. 13 years ago, I became a Mom and home cook. Altering my skills to the simple and picky. From making baby food to homemade breads and casseroles. During those 12 years, I joined the cupcake and personal cake craze, cookie trays, catering and luncheons. I have worked the past 4 years as a personal Chef. Tightening my finite skills in taste, nutrition, and presentation.

So with over 25 years of a variety of experience and experiences, my most favorite thing to do is to take what is in my head and share and show people about food. I have worked to empower my local community by volunteering with community gardening events, church cook-offs, Life-Skills classes for autistic learners, and question and answer forums. I don't believe in the cliché, "I can't cook, I even burn water." Anybody can learn through trial and error and become more independent through being able to feed themselves and their loved ones.

This is my Cookbook for you to Journal and make into your Cookbook. You can keep it simple or really experiment. The choice and Journey is yours. Just write down everything because as much as we'd like to remember everything later....